ACID RAIN

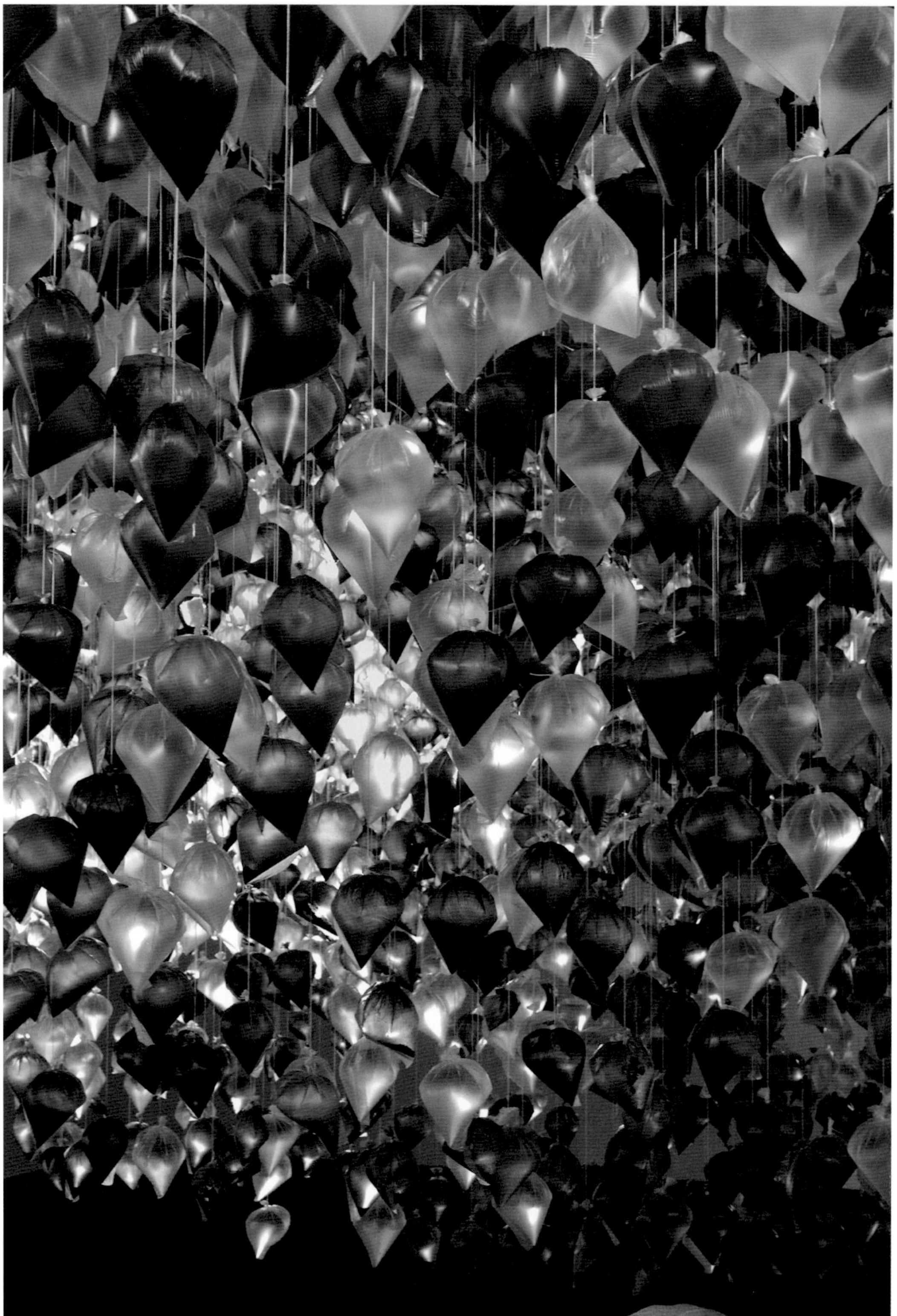

Bright Ugochukwu Eke, *Clouds-Earth Twist*, Ursula Blickle Stiftung, 2013

ACID RAIN

BRIGHT UGOCHUKWU EKE

Clouds-Earth Twist

URSULA BLICKLE STIFTUNG

jovis art

„Ich war im Süden Nigerias unterwegs, im Nigerdelta. Eine Region, die von der Ölindustrie geprägt ist. Alle großen internationalen Konzerne fördern dort das Schwarze Gold. Zwei Tage nachdem es geregnet hatte, bekam ich heftigen Hautausschlag. Ein Arzt sagte mir, dass das eine Reaktion auf den verseuchten Regen sei. Das hat mir wirklich Angst eingejagt, aber es hat mich auch dazu inspiriert, mit Wasser zu arbeiten und mich intensiv mit Umweltthemen zu beschäftigen."

Bright Ugochukwu Eke

CLOUDS-EARTH TWIST

ALFRED WEIDINGER

„Sauerer Regen", ein mir heute noch durch Mark und Bein gehender Begriff für ein in den 1980er Jahren kolportiertes Schreckensszenario, demnach es in weiten Teilen Europas und Nordamerikas bald keinen Wald mehr geben sollte. In Deutschland nährte vor allem das Hochglanzmagazin „Stern" die sich rasch verbreitende Hysterie durch einen im November 1981 erschienen Beitrag „Über allen Wipfeln ist Gift" und damit dem Start seiner später preisgekrönten Reihe „Saurer Regen über Deutschland – Der Wald stirbt". Das Trauma hat zwar in meinem Unterbewusstsein einen Platz gefunden. In der öffentlichen Wahrnehmung aber ist das Schreckgespenst „Saurer Regen" mittlerweile gänzlich verschwunden.
Aber was wurde eigentlich aus dem Waldsterben? War die Gefahr für die Wälder wirklich so groß – oder war es bloße Medienhysterie? Der Wald ist nicht gestorben! Im Gegenteil, er ist größer geworden. Mehr als 30 Jahre nach den hitzigen Diskussionen um das Waldsterben durch sauren Regen erstreckt sich der deutsche Wald heute über elf Millionen Hektar, eine Million Hektar mehr als 1983. Faktum ist: Die Gefahr für den Wald wurde übertrieben dargestellt. Faktum ist aber auch: Die emotionale Diskussion hat dazu geführt, dass entschiedenere Gesetze zur Rauchgasentschwefelung verabschiedet wurden. Denn ungefilterte Emissionen aus Industrie, Heizungen und Verkehr hatten sich seit den 1950er Jahren mehr als verdoppelt. Selbst in den industriefernen Regionen wurden damals hundertfach überhöhte Schwermetall- und Schwefelsäurekonzentrationen gemessen. Bis weit in die 1990 er Jahre galt daher ein großer Teil der Umweltschutzanstrengungen dem Kampf gegen den sauren Regen. Gesetzliche Normen und der verpflichtende Einsatz von Anlagen zur Rauchgasentschwefelung und Katalysatoren zeigte über die Jahre Wirkung. Dennoch wurde bis zum gegenwärtigen Zeitpunkt kein Alleinschuldiger für den damals tatsächlich schlechten Zustand der Wälder (die Spuren sind beispielsweise im *Nationalpark Bayerischer Wald* heute noch erkennbar) identifiziert.

Wenn ich mich an bedeutende Umweltkatastrophen erinnere fällt mir allerdings nicht nur saurer Regen ein. Abgesehen von der Nuklearkatastrophe von

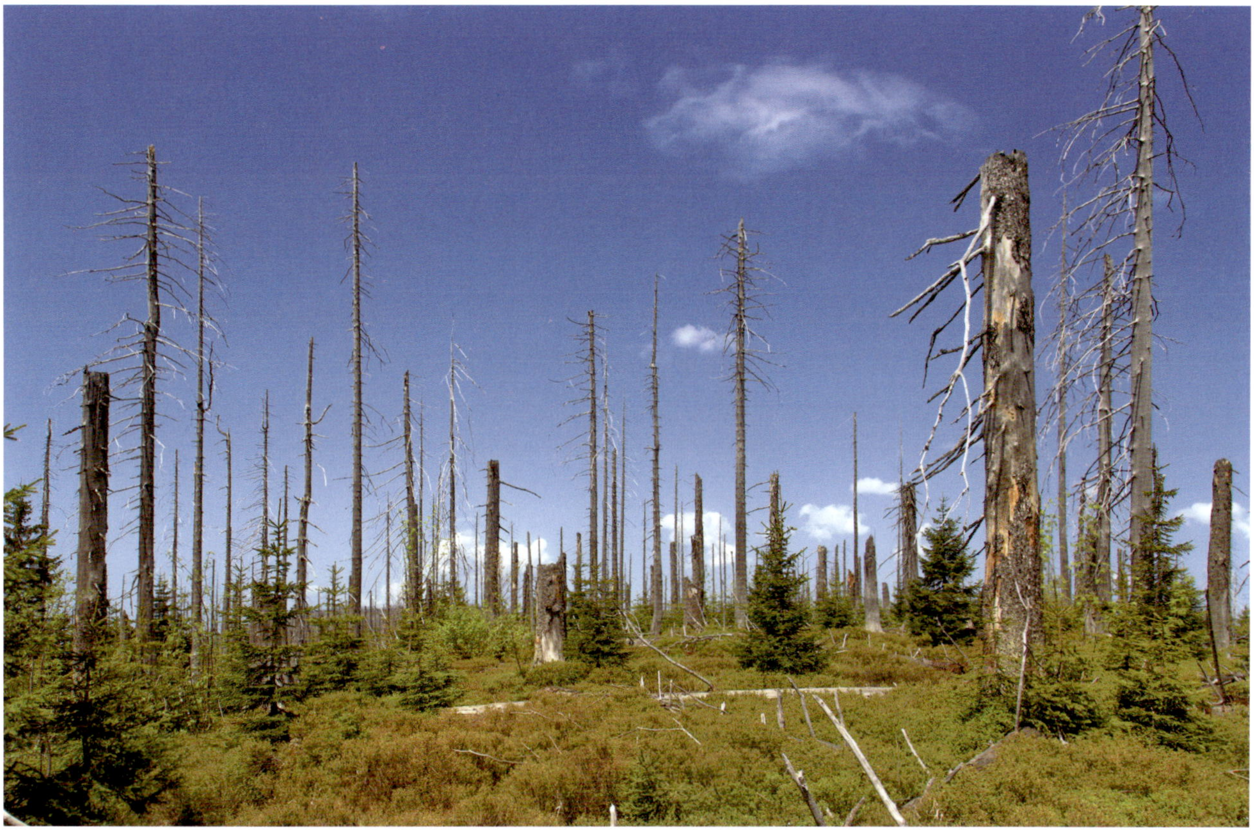

Waldsterben im Nationalpark Bayerischer Wald, 2013
Forest dieback in the Bavarian National Park, 2013
Foto/Photo: Karl Bloch

Tschernobyl in 1986 denke ich vor allem an den unter US-amerikanischer Flagge fahrenden und 1989 auf Grund gelaufenen Supertanker *Exxon Valdez*. Damals ergossen sich 40 Millionen Liter Erdöl ins Meer und bis heute ist die Flora, Fauna und überhaupt der ganze Küstenabschnitt schwer belastet. Monatelang berichteten die internationalen Medien vom Ausmaß der Katastrophe und veröffentlichten Bilder von ölverschmierten qualvoll zu Grunde gehenden Tieren. Die Krise machte *Exxon* zur Zielscheibe von protestierenden Umweltschützern, von Politikern und Medien; die Kosten für die Reinigung der Gewässer und die Schadensersatzzahlungen waren gewaltig. Außerdem büßte der Konzern große Teile seiner jährlichen Einnahmen durch einen weltweiten Boykott ein. Das Image von *Exxon* war zu dieser Zeit und noch lange danach stark beschädigt; der Name *Exxon* galt Ende der 1980er Jahre als Synonym für einen ökologisch völlig unverantwortlich agierenden Konzern.

Aber was ist mit dem das Unglück der *Exxon Valdez* weit in den Schatten stellende, und mittlerweile seit genau 55 Jahren andauernde, Umweltdesaster im nigerianischen Niger-Delta? Wo bleiben die internationalen Proteste angesichts der dahin siechenden Umwelt? Experten schätzen, dass seit dem Beginn der Ölförderung 1958 etwa 13 Millionen Barrel (etwas mehr als 1,5 Milliarden Liter) Öl im Niger-Delta, dem wichtigstes Erdölfördergebiet Nigerias, unkontrolliert ausgeflossen sind. Nahezu alle bekannten Ölkonzerne sind dort tätig. Die allgemeine Untätigkeit erinnert mich an das anfängliche Achselzucken in der Zeit des über Europa sich ergießenden sauren Regens, weil man doch gegen ihn und die Übermacht der Konzerne machtlos war.

Das Niger-Delta ist die Heimat von mehr als 30 Millionen Menschen und gilt als eines der weltweit wichtigsten Ökosysteme. Es ist das größte Feuchtgebiet Nigerias und besteht aus Mangrovenwäldern, Süßwassersümpfen und Tieflandregenwäldern. Doch große Teile werden von öligem Wasser und toten Fischen in einer sterbenden Natur dominiert. Das Abfackeln von Gasresten ist zwar verboten, dennoch erhellen unzählige Gasfackeln die Nächte im Niger-Delta und der ungefilterte Austrag aus giftigen, gesundheitsschädlichen oder umweltgefährdenden chemischen Stoffen

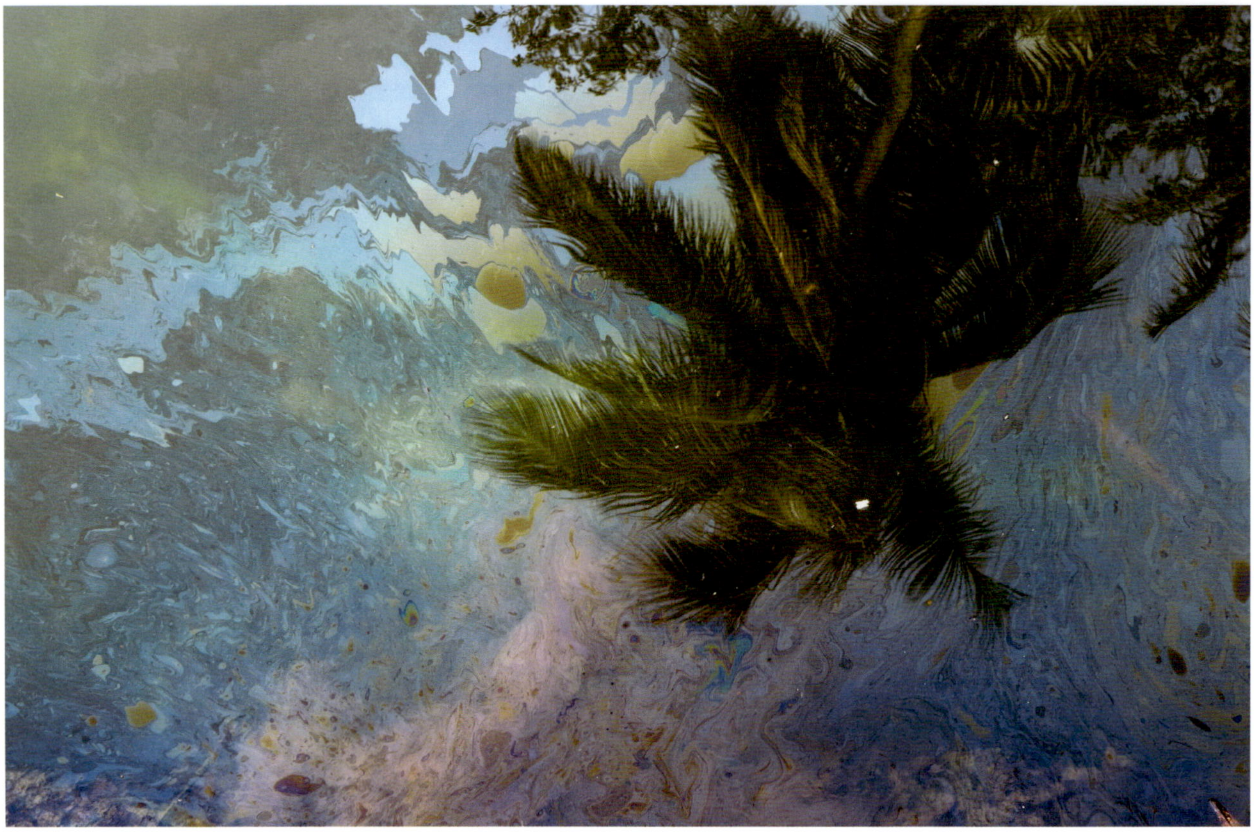

Öl-Industrie im Niger Delta, Nigeria, 2008
Im September 2007 ereignete sich eine große Öl-Katastrophe (Shell) nahe von Goi in Ongoniland.

The Oil Industry in the Niger Delta, Nigeria, 2008
In September 2007 a big oil spill (Shell) occurred near the community of Goi, Ongoniland.

Foto/Photo: Kadir van Lohuizen

verunreinigt seit Jahrzehnten die Luft. Obwohl Vandalismus und Diebstahl eine Mitschuld an der Misere tragen sind die Ölgesellschaften (beteiligte Konzerne sind Shell, Chevron, ExxonMobil und Total) für die überwiegende Mehrheit der Leckagen und berstenden Bohrköpfe verantwortlich. 2009 hat Amnesty International den dramatischen Bericht *Petroleum, Pollution and Poverty in the Niger Delta* veröffentlicht. Die Studie macht unter anderem auf Ölverschmutzungen – gemäß Shell werden 50 Prozent der Leckagen auf ihrem Gebiet durch Korrosion verursacht – und das Abfackeln von Gas aufmerksam und warnt eindringlich vor den fatalen Folgen für Mensch und Umwelt. Die Bewohner des Niger-Delta trinken, kochen und waschen mit verschmutztem Wasser, essen mit Erdöl verseuchten Fisch und nehmen mit den Nahrungsmitteln Giftstoffe zu sich. Dementsprechend beträgt die Lebenserwartung der im Niger-Delta lebenden Bevölkerung derzeit nur mehr 41 Jahre.

Der 1976 in Mbaise im Niger-Delta geborene Künstler Bright Ugochukwu Eke erlitt als Folge eines in der nigerianischen Ölstadt Port Harcourt sich ereignenden toxischen Niederschlags eine Hautinfektion, die ihn später zu einer intensiven künstlerischen Auseinandersetzung inspirierte. An der *Faculty of Arts* der *University of Nigeria* in Nsukka zum Bildhauer ausgebildet trifft er auf den dort lehrenden ghanaischen Bildhauer El Anatsui der zu seinem bedeutendsten Mentor wird. Anatsui, ein Mitglied der sog. Nsukka-Gruppe, beginnt sich während Bright´s Studienzeit mit Wand-Installationen aus recycelten Materialien (vorzugsweise zusammengepresste Weißbleche und Aluminium) auseinanderzusetzen, die er zu monumentalen, *gawk* („Metall" oder „altmodisches Tuch") genannten „Stoffbahnen" verwebt. Bewusst assoziiert er diese Assemblagen mit den aufwändig gewebten Kente-Tüchern der ghanaischen Könige (vor allem der Ewe-Kultur) und verwebt mit seiner Geschichte konnotierte Aspekte der nigerianischen und ghanaischen Kunst und Kultur mit den ökologischen Problemen Westafrikas. In diesem künstlerischen Umfeld entwickelt Bright auf der Grundlage seiner körperlichen Erfahrung und des erlebten und allgegenwärti-

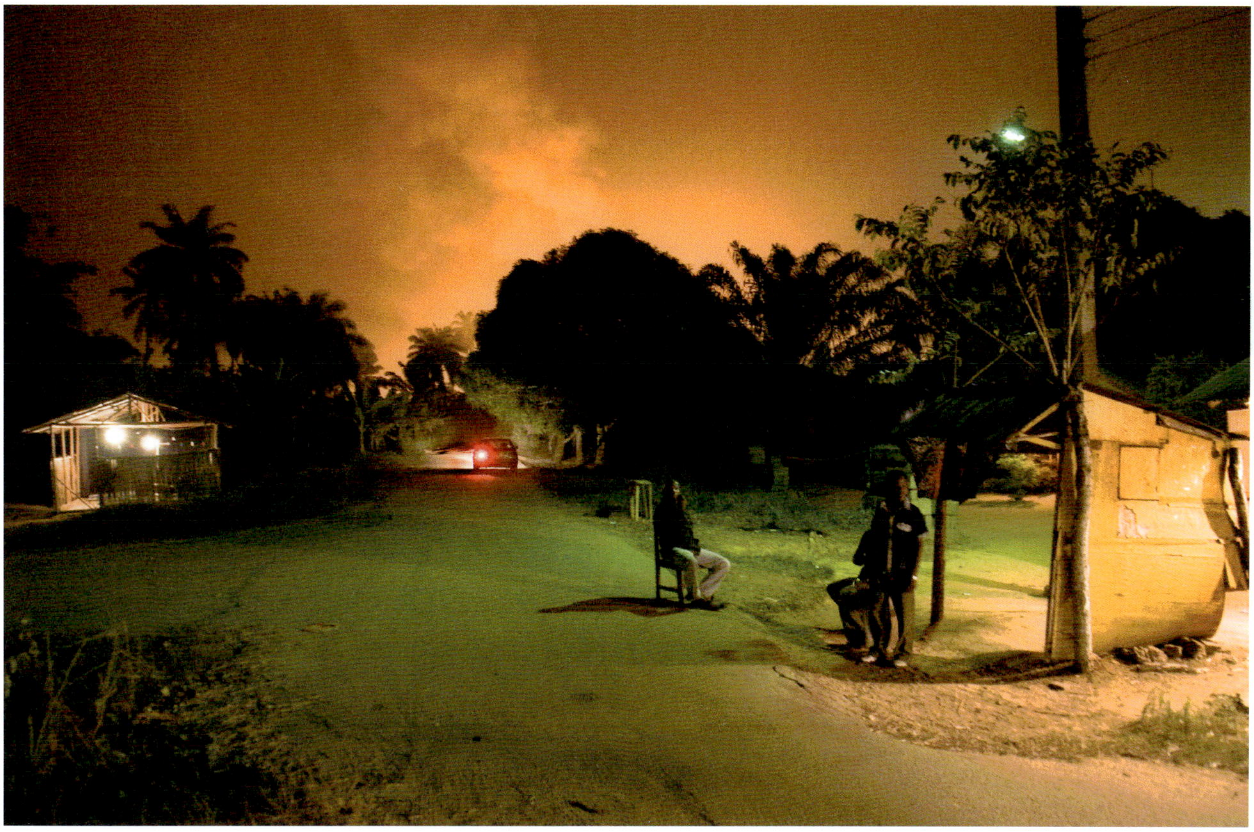

Öl-Industrie im Niger Delta, Nigeria, 2008
Eine orange-rote Agip-Gasflamme erleuchtet den Himmel über Akala-Olu im Niger Delta.
Die Flammen brennen immerwährend, für die Einwohner wird es niemals Nacht.

The Oil Industry in the Niger Delta, Nigeria, 2008
The orange glow from a gasflare from Agip shines in the community of Akala-Olu in Nigeria.
Flares burn continuously, and for people living nearby, night never really comes.

Foto/Photo: Kadir van Lohuizen

gen Umweltdesasters in seiner Heimat für die Dak´Art (Dakar Biennale of Contemporary African Art) 2006 eine zweiteilige Installation mit dem bezeichnenden Titel *Acid Rain* (Saurer Regen). Der Titel unterstreicht die Faszination, die das Grundelement Wasser auf den Künstler ausübt und seine Unentbehrlichkeit für jegliches Leben auf diesem Planeten. So prosaisch der Titel im Moment seiner ersten Wahrnehmung sein mag, so sehr ist das Werk eine Reaktion auf die vollkommene Missachtung der Umwelt sowohl durch die nigerianischen Behörden, den im Niger-Delta Erdöl fördernden Konzernen als auch den gedankenlosen Bewohnern, die einen nicht unwesentlichen Beitrag zur Verschmutzung und Zerstörung ihres Lebensraumes beisteuern. Das wohl wesentlichste Element dieser Installation ist ein *Acid Rain* benanntes Werk, die sich aus einer Unzahl von kleinen, mit Wasser und Ammoniumchlorid (Salmiak) gefüllten Plastiktüten zusammensetzt. Bright arrangiert die Installation im Bereich der Tropfkante eines Daches und evoziert damit den Eindruck von der Dachkante fließender Regentropfen. Das auf toxischen Regen im Niger-Delta und damit auf seine eigene Lebensgeschichte hinweisende Werk ergänzt Bright durch die raumgreifende Installation *Shield*. Für dieses metaphernreiche Werk vernähte Bright die in Westafrika üblicherweise von Straßenhändlern angebotenen Plastiksäckchen mit Trinkwasser zu vor saurem Regen schützenden Regenschutzmänteln und Regenschirmen. Im Jahr darauf zeigt Bright in der Ausstellung *Environ-Scope* des Goethe-Instituts in Lagos eine weitere Form von *Acid Rain*. Wie bereits in Dakar werden mit kontaminiertem Wasser gefüllte Plastiksäckchen im Freien aufgehängt. Um das Thema der Installation noch deutlicher zu veranschaulichen, entschließt sich Bright sein Werk an den Ästen eines Baumes anzubringen, wo es den Eindruck von nach dem Regen herabperlenden Wassertropfen erweckt. 2008 konzipiert Bright für die Ausstellung *ECho Wanted* der Galerie Karsten Greve in Paris eine formale Weiterentwicklung von *Acid Rain*. Dazu bilden etwas mehr als 3000 von der Raumdecke abgehängte und mit Kohlepulver versehene Wassersäckchen die Form eines großen Wassertropfens (*Water*

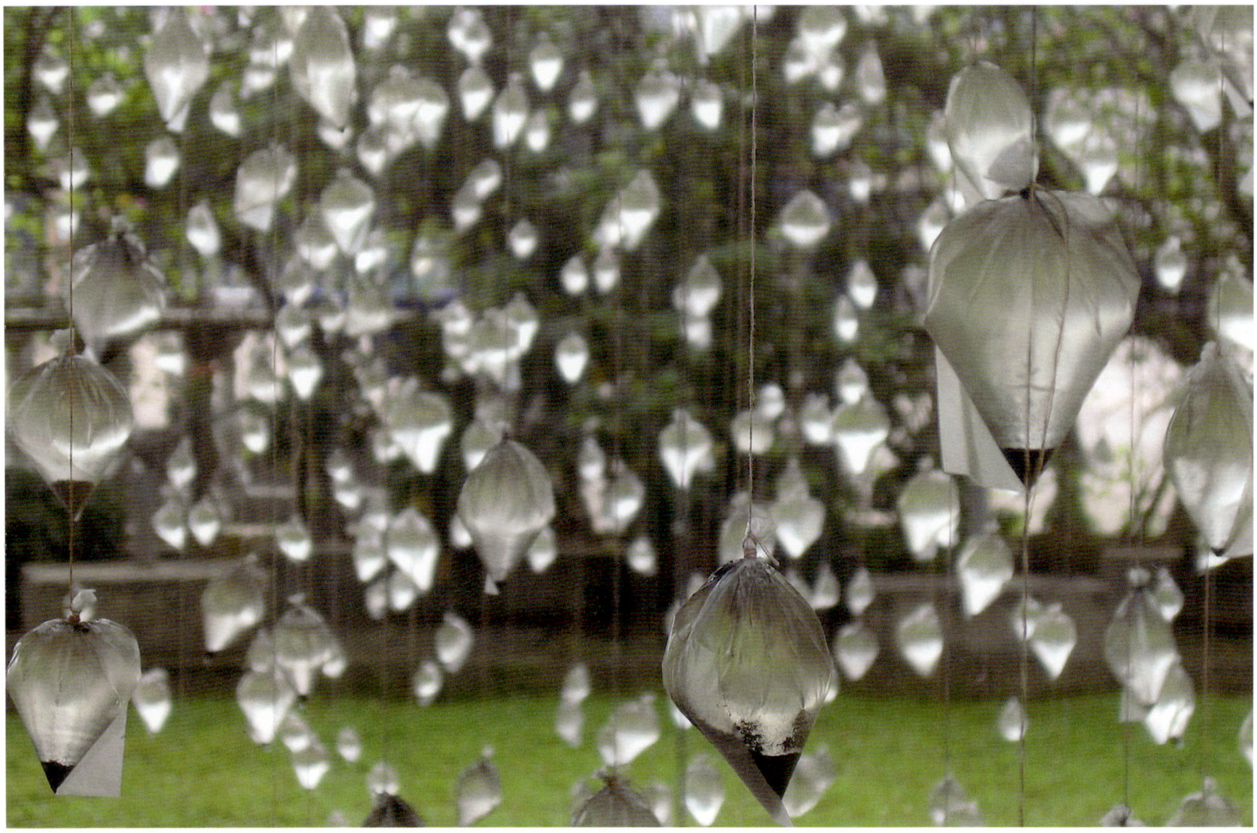

Bright Ugochukwu Eke, *Acid Rain*, Goethe Institut, Lagos, 2007

Drop). 2009 ermöglicht das Frie Centre in Kopenhagen im Zusammenhang mit der Gruppenausstellung *Contemporary Art and Climate Change* dem Künstler eine aus mehr als 10.000 Teilen bestehende, raumgreifende Installation von *Acid Rain* zu produzieren. Bright führt dafür sein Werk in der Form eines sphärisch wirkenden Sprühnebels aus. Dieses formale Konzept setzt er später auch im niederländischen s´-Hertogenbosch (*The woods that see and hear*) und im Palazzo della Gran Guardia in Verona (*What´s the Matter?*) um. In Form einer Wolke zeigt Bright weitere Versionen von *Acid Rain* in einer anlässlich des UN-Klimagipfels von der Durban Art Gallery 2011 gezeigten Installation *Between Earth and Clouds* sowie als *Heavy Clouds* in der im selben Jahr im Åland Konstmuseum in Finnland organisierten Gruppenausstellung *ARS11 - WATER & WASTE*.

Mit der im September 2013 für die Ursula Blickle Stiftung konzipierten Installation *Clouds-Earth Twist* bezieht sich Bright auf ein 2005 in Nigeria entstandenes Werk *Heaven and Earth*, in dem er mit Spiegeln den Himmel und die Erde in einen künstlerischen Zusammenhang bringt. In formaler Hinsicht greift er die vor zwei Jahren in Durban gezeigte Installation *Between Earth and Clouds* auf und entwickelt sie für die Ursula Blickle Stiftung weiter. Erstmals setzt Bright die zwei sein Werk dominierenden Grundelemente Wasser und Erde auf physisch zueinander in Beziehung. Die in der Raummitte situierte Regenwolke findet ihre formale Entsprechung im unter ihr aufgeschütteten Sandhaufen. Das Zusammentreffen der beiden Elemente veranschaulicht ihre überlebensnotwendige Symbiose. Die Form der Sanduhr ist nicht zufällig entstanden: Genau vor 55 Jahren wurde im Niger-Delta der Grundstein für eine der größten Umweltkatastrophen dieser Erde gelegt. Wie lange die Zeit für wirksame Gegenmaßnahmen und Handlungen noch ausreicht verrät der Blick auf die Installation *Clouds-Earth Twist* von Bright Ugochukwu Eke nicht, aber sie gemahnt daran sich eines der größten Umweltdesaster unserer Zeit zu vergegenwärtigen und daran zu erinnern, dass es irgendwann einmal zu spät sein wird.

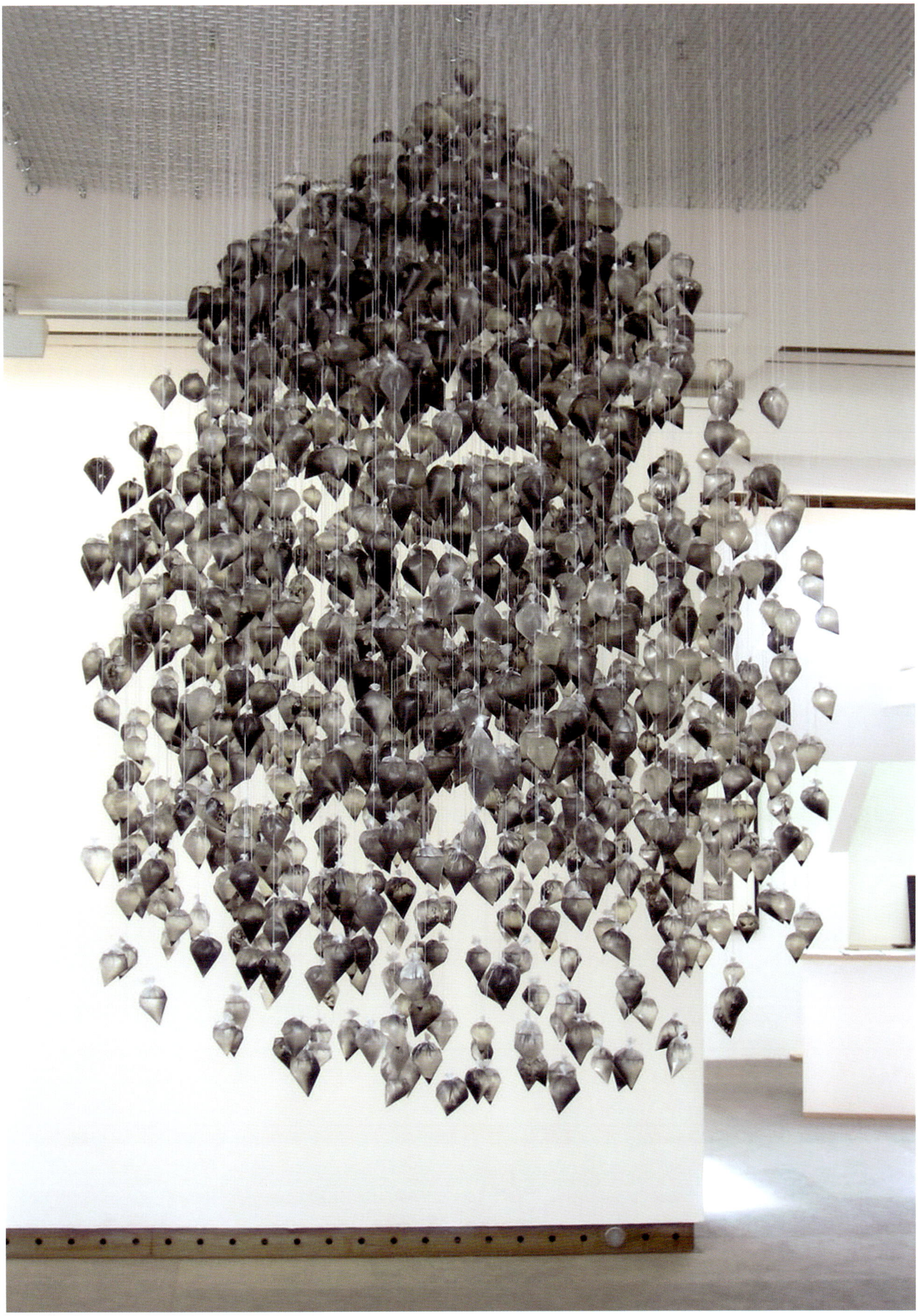

Bright Ugochukwu Eke, *Water Drop*, Galerie Karsten Greve, Paris 2008

"I was travelling through the Niger Delta in southern Nigeria – a region where the oil industry has left its mark. All the big international oil concerns extract "black gold" here. Two days after it had rained I developed a severe skin rash. The doctor told me it was a reaction to the polluted rain. That really scared me, but it also inspired me to work with water and to make an intensive study of environmental themes."

Bright Ugochukwu Eke

CLOUDS-EARTH TWIST

ALFRED WEIDINGER

"Acid rain" is an expression which still sends shivers down my spine. It describes a horror scenario which was current during the 1980s and which claimed that before long forests would cease to exist in extensive parts of Europe and North America. In Germany it was primarily the glossy magazine *Stern* that fanned the rapidly spreading hysteria with an article published in November 1981 entitled "Über allen Wipfeln ist Gift" (Poison in the Tree-Tops), which marked the start of its series "Saurer Regen über Deutschland – Der Wald stirbt" (Acid Rain over Germany – the Forest is Dying), which later won a number of awards. The trauma engraved itself into my subconscious; however, the nightmare of "acid rain" has since completely vanished from public awareness.
But what happened to the dying forests? Were they really in such danger, or was it just media hysteria? The forest did not die! Quite the opposite – it has grown in size. More than thirty years after the heated discussions about the death of the forest as a result of acid rain, German forests today cover more than eleven million hectares, one million more than in 1983. The fact is: the danger to the forests was exaggerated. But it is also a fact that the emotional discussion resulted in stricter laws about smoke desulphurisation being passed, because unfiltered emissions from industry, heating and traffic have also more than doubled since the 1950s. Even in non-industrial regions, the concentrations of heavy metals and sulphuric acid that were measured were more than one hundred times higher in those days. Until well into the 1990s, therefore, a major part of the environmental effort was directed towards the fight against acid rain. Over the years the legal limits and the compulsory use of desulphurisation plants and catalytic converters had an effect. Nonetheless, up to the present time no single factor has been identified as being responsible for the condition of the forests, which really was poor in those days (and traces can still be seen to this day in the *Bavarian Forest National Park*, for example).

When I look back on important environmental disasters, however, I find myself thinking not only of acid rain. Apart from the nuclear catastrophe of Chernobyl

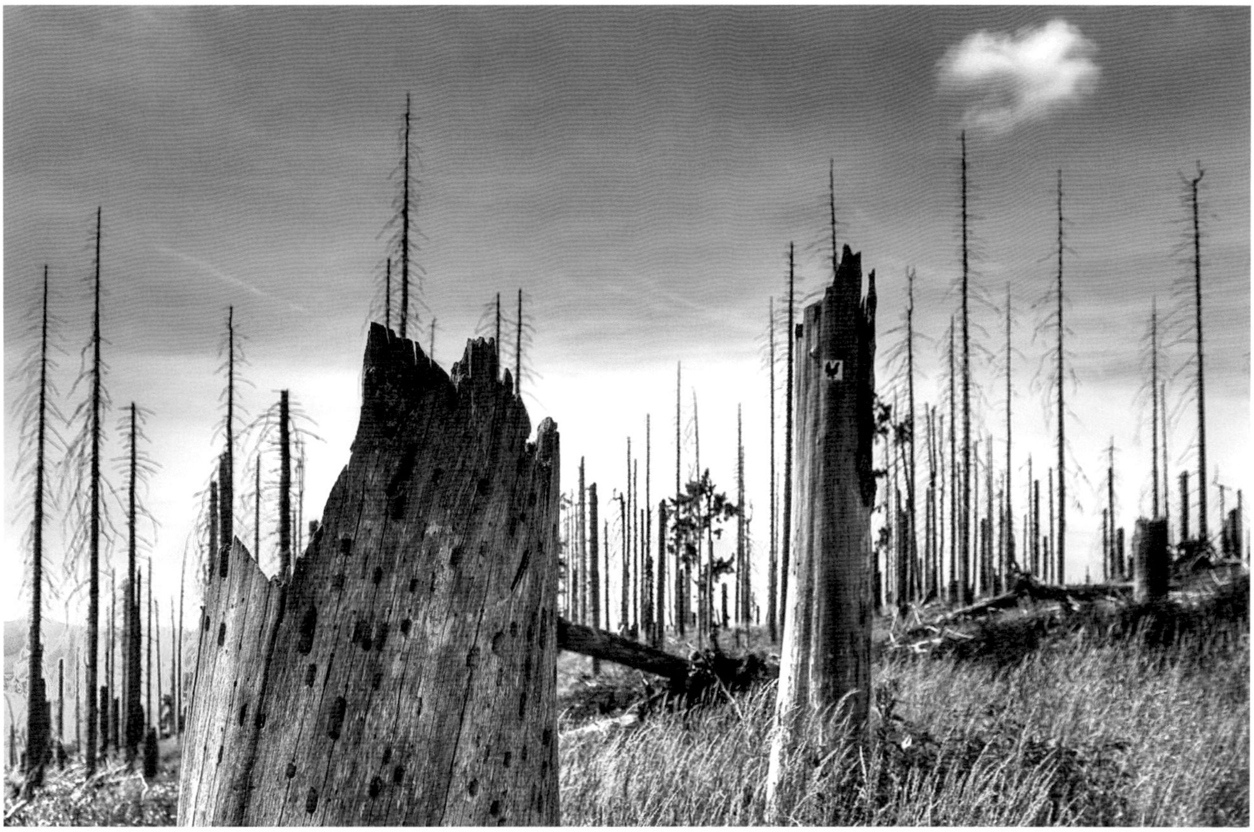

Waldsterben im Nationalpark Bayerischer Wald, 2006
Forest dieback in the Bavarian National Park, 2006
Foto/Photo: Christian Mistelbach

in 1986, above all I think of the supertanker *Exxon Valdez*, which sailed under the American flag and which ran aground in 1989. Forty million litres of crude oil flowed into the sea at the time, and to this day the vegetation and wildlife, the entire stretch of coastline in fact, are still heavily polluted. For months the international media reported the extent of the catastrophe and published pictures of birds and animals covered in oil and dying in agony. The crisis made the *Exxon* the target of protesting environmental activists, politicians and the media; the costs of cleaning up the waters and compensation payments were huge. Moreover, the concern lost a large part of its annual revenues as the result of a worldwide boycott. The image of *Exxon* was badly damaged not only at the time but for a long time afterwards; at the end of the 1980s the name *Exxon* was a synonym for a company that operated in a totally irresponsible manner from an ecological point of view. But what about the environmental disaster in the Niger Delta in Nigeria, which has already lasted for exactly 55 years and which eclipses the *Exxon Valdez* accident by far? Where are the international protests at the way the environment is being destroyed? Experts estimate that since the beginning of oil production in 1958 some 13 million barrels of oil (somewhat more than 1.5 billion litres) have flowed in an uncontrolled manner into the Niger Delta, the most important oil-producing region of Nigeria. Almost all the best-known oil concerns are operating there. The general lack of activity reminds me of the way that at the beginning people merely shrugged their shoulders at the acid rain that was pouring down onto Europe, because they thought they were powerless in the face of the problem and the overriding power of industry. The Niger Delta is home to more than 30 million people and is regarded as one of the world's most important ecosystems. It is the biggest wetland area in Nigeria and consists of mangrove forests, freshwater swamps and lowland rainforest. But large sections are full of water polluted with oil and dead fish in a nature that is inexorably dying. The torching of gas residues is banned, and yet at night countless gas flares light up the Niger Delta, and for decades the air there has been polluted by the unfiltered emission of toxic chemical substances which are

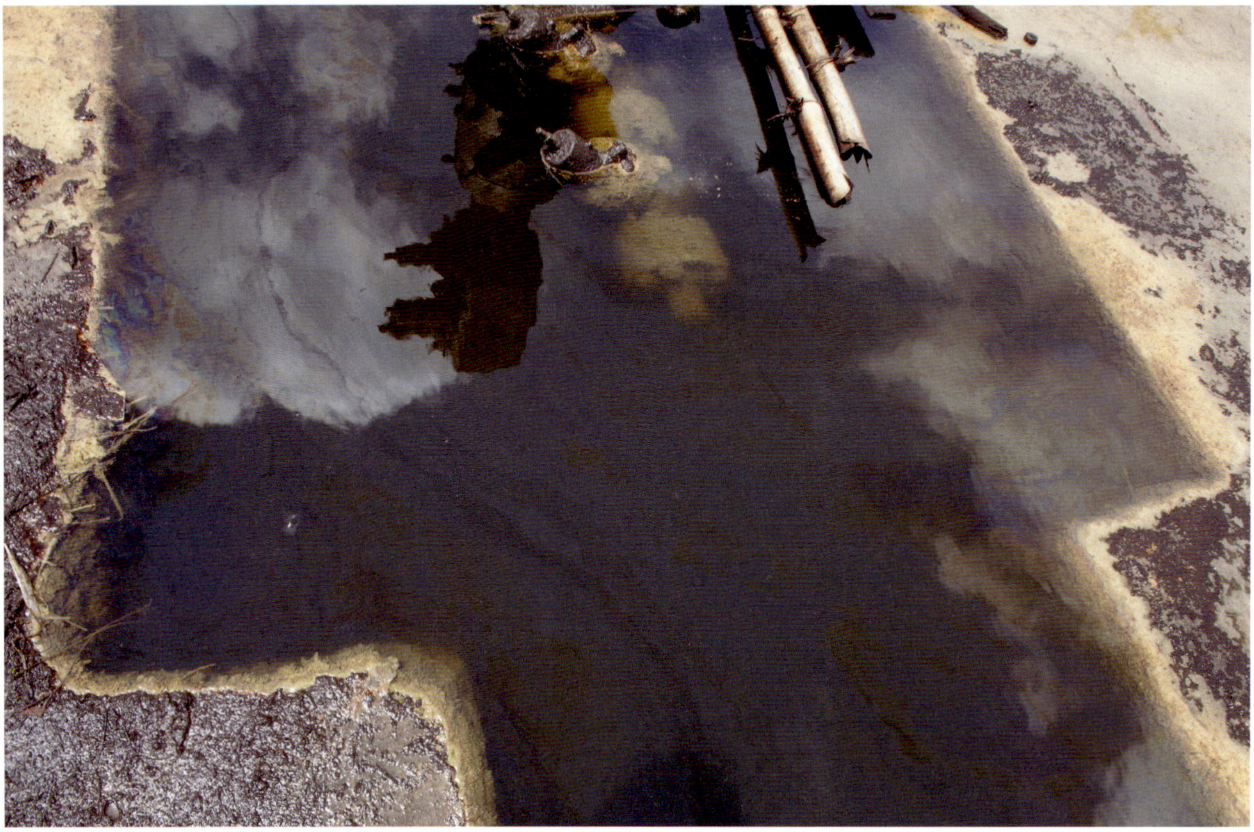

Ölpest im Niger Delta, Kegbara Dere, Nigeria, 2010
Defekte Bohrlochköpfe als Verursacher einer dramatischen Ölpest in Kegbara Dere, Nigeria, 50 km von Port Harcourt entfernt.

Niger Delta Oil Spill, Kegbara Dere, Nigeria, 2010
Oil well heads on land devasted from an oil spill in Kegbara Dere, Nigeria, 50 km from Port Harcourt.

Foto/Photo: Jane Hahn/Corbis

damaging to health or dangerous for the environment. Although vandalism and theft must take part of the blame for the misery, it is the oil companies (including Shell, Chevron, ExxonMobil and Total) that are responsible for by far the majority of the leaks and burst drilling heads. In 2009 Amnesty International published the dramatic report *Petroleum, Pollution and Poverty in the Niger Delta*. The study draws attention, amongst other things, to oil pollution – according to Shell, 50 percent of the leaks within their region are caused by corrosion – and to the torching of gas. It also issued an urgent warning about the fatal consequences for both humankind and the environment. The inhabitants of the Niger Delta use the polluted water for drinking, cooking and washing; they eat fish polluted with oil and thus consume poisons along with their food. Accordingly, the expectation of life for the population living in the Niger Delta is currently only 41 years.

The artist Bright Ugochukwu Eke was born in 1976 in Mbaise in Eastern Nigeria. As the result of acid rain that fell in the oil-producing city of Port Harcourt in Nigeria he developed a skin infection which later inspired him to make an intensive study in his art. During his training as a sculptor at the *Faculty of Arts* of the *University of Nigeria* in Nsukka, he met the Ghanaian sculptor El Anatsui, who was a lecturer there and who became his most important mentor. During Bright's time as a student Anatsui, a member of the so-called Nsukka Group, began to work with wall installations of recycled materials (especially compressed tin plate and aluminium), which he wove into monumental "lengths of fabric" known as *gawk* (which mans "metal" or "old-fashioned cloth"). He deliberately associated these assemblages with the elaborately woven *kente* cloths worn by the kings of Ghana (especially in the Ewe culture), interweaving through its historical associations specific aspects of Nigerian and Ghanaian art and culture with the ecological problems of West Africa. It was within this artistic environment that Bright developed a two-part installation with the significant title *Acid Rain* (Saurer Regen), based on his physical experience and the environmental disaster in his homeland which could be seen and experienced all around, for

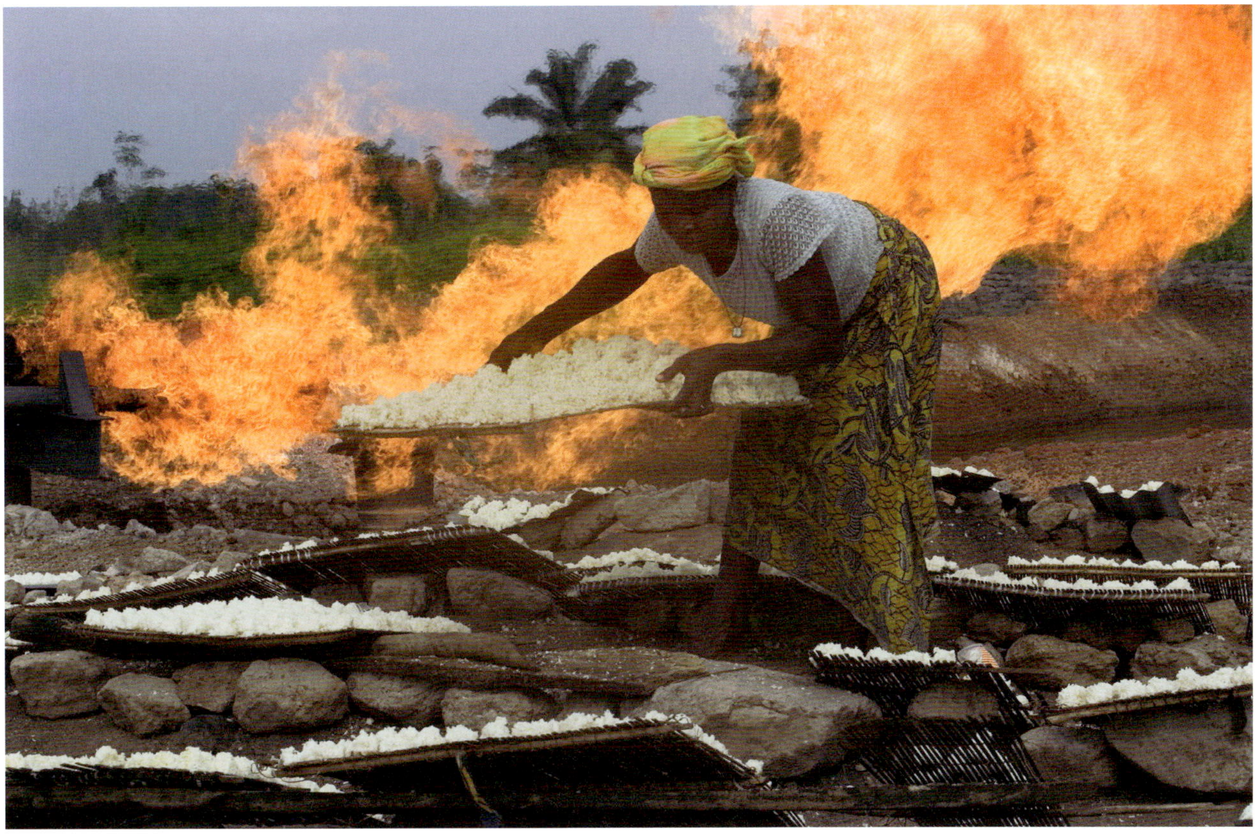

Ölpest im Niger Delta, Aflesere, Warri North, Nigeria, 2004
Die Urohobo backen "krokpo-garri" oder Tapioka in der Hitze einer Gasflamme. Die Lebensdauer dieser Menschen ist sehr kurz, Schadstoffe aus den Gasflammen führen zu schweren gesundheitlichen Problemen.

Niger Delta Oil Spill, Aflesere, Warri North, Nigeria, 2004
Local Urohobo people bake "krokpo-garri", or tapioca in the heat of a gas flare. Life span is short for these people, as pollutants from the flare cause serious health problems.

Foto/Photo: Ed Kashi/VII/Corbis

the Dak'Art (Dakar Biennale of Contemporary African Art) in 2006. The title of Bright's work underlines the fascination which the basic element water exerts on the artist and its indispensability for all forms of life on the planet. The title may appear prosaic at first sight, but the work is a reaction to the complete disregard for the environment by the Nigerian authorities, the companies producing oil in the Niger Delta and the thoughtless inhabitants, who make a not insignificant contribution to the pollution and destruction of their environment. The essential element in the installation is a work entitled *Acid Rain* which is made up of a vast number of small plastic bags filled with water mixed with ammonium chloride. Bright arranged the installation near the gutter of a roof, thereby evoking the impression of raindrops running off a roof. The work draws attention to the acid rain in the Niger Delta and hence to his own biography. Bright complements the work by his space-consuming installation *Shield*. For this work, which is rich in metaphors, Bright stitched together the plastic bags which are usually used by street hawkers selling drinking water in West Africa in order to create protective raincoats and umbrellas against the acid rain. The following year Bright showed another form of *Acid Rain* in the exhibition *EnvironScope* staged by the Goethe Institute in Lagos. As previously in Dakar he suspended plastic bags filled with contaminated water in the open air. In order to make the subject of the installation even clearer, however, Bright decided to suspend the work from the branches of a tree, where it created the impression of water dripping down after the rain. In 2008 Bright devised a further development of the form of *Acid Rain* for the exhibition *ECho Wanted* at the Galerie Karsten Greve in Paris. Here more than 3,000 bags of water to which charcoal powder had been added were suspended from the ceiling of the room in the form of a huge drop of water (*Water Drop*). In 2009, in connection with the group exhibition *Contemporary Art and Climate Change* the Frie Centre in Copenhagen enabled the artist to produce an extensive installation of *Acid Rain* consisting of more than 10,000 parts. In this case Bright created his work in the form of a spray mist which seemed to form a sphere. He subsequently also

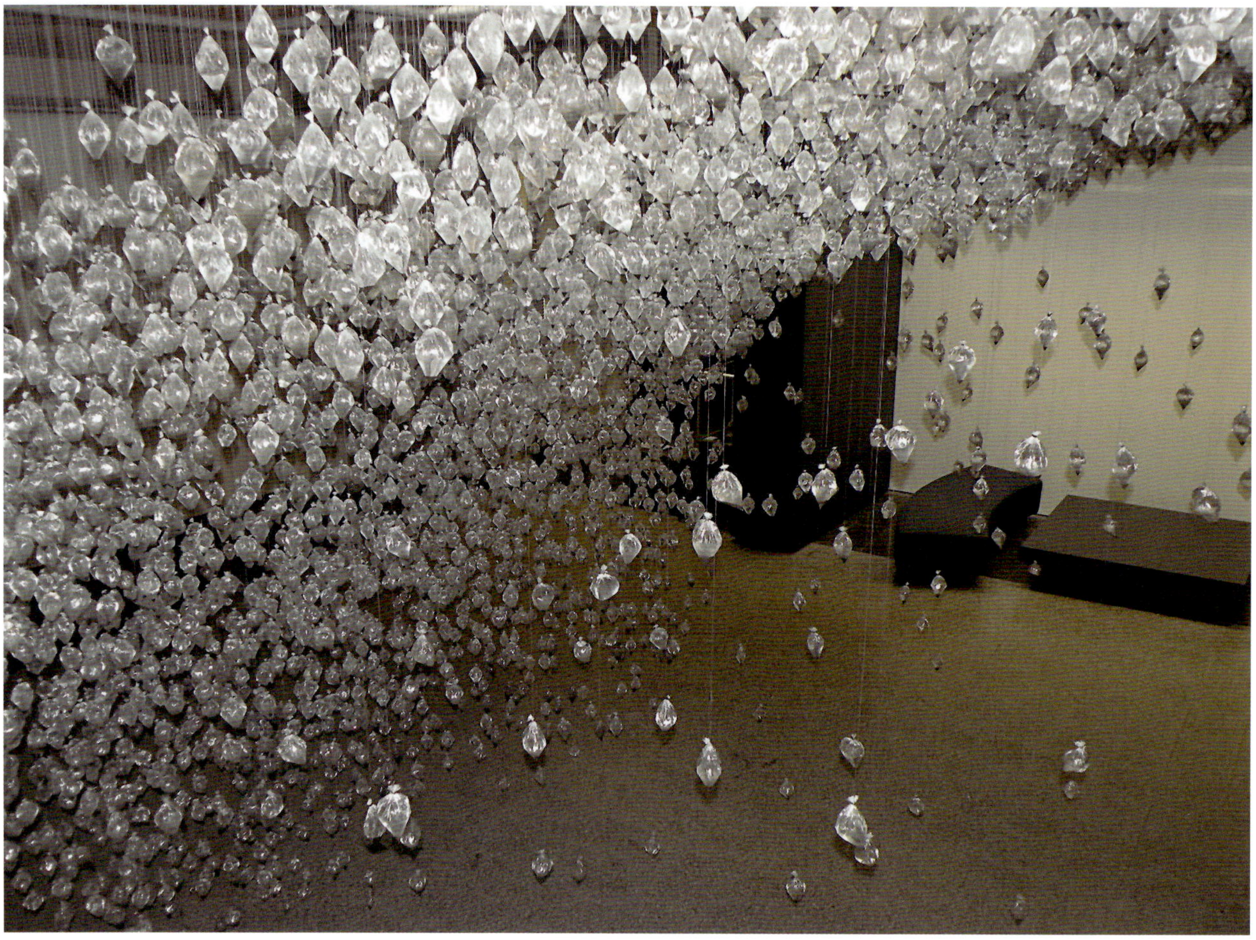

Bright Ugochukwu Eke, *Heavy Clouds*, Alands Konstmuseum, Finland/Finnland

implemented this formal concept in s'Hertogenbosch in the Netherlands (*The woods that see and hear*) and in the Palazzo della Gran Guardia in Verona (*What's the Matter?*). Bright showed further versions of *Acid Rain* in the form of a cloud in an installation entitled *Between Earth and Clouds* at the Durban Art Gallery on the occasion of the UN climate summit in 2011, and during the same year with the title *Heavy Clouds* as part of the group exhibition *ARS11 - WATER & WASTE* in the Åland Konstmuseum in Finland.

With the installation *Clouds-Earth Twist* devised in September 2013 for the Ursula Blickle Foundation, Bright refers to *Heaven and Earth*, a work created in 2005 in Nigeria. In this work he used mirrors to create an artistic connection between the sky and the earth. With regard to the form of the work, he takes up the installation *Between Earth and Clouds* which was shown two years previously in Durban, now continuing its development for the Ursula Blickle Foundation. First of all Bright establishes a physical connection between the two basic elements which dominate his work, water and earth. The rain cloud in the centre of the room is echoed formally by the heap of sand piled up beneath it. The encounter between these two elements demonstrates their symbiosis which is essential for survival. The form of the sand glass is not arbitrary: exactly 55 years ago in the Niger Delta, the foundation stone was laid for one of the biggest environmental disasters on Earth. How much time remains for effective counter-measures and action is not revealed by the installation *Clouds-Earth Twist* by Bright Ugochukwu Eke, but it does demand that we should be aware of the greatest environmental disasters of our time and it reminds us that one day it really will be too late.

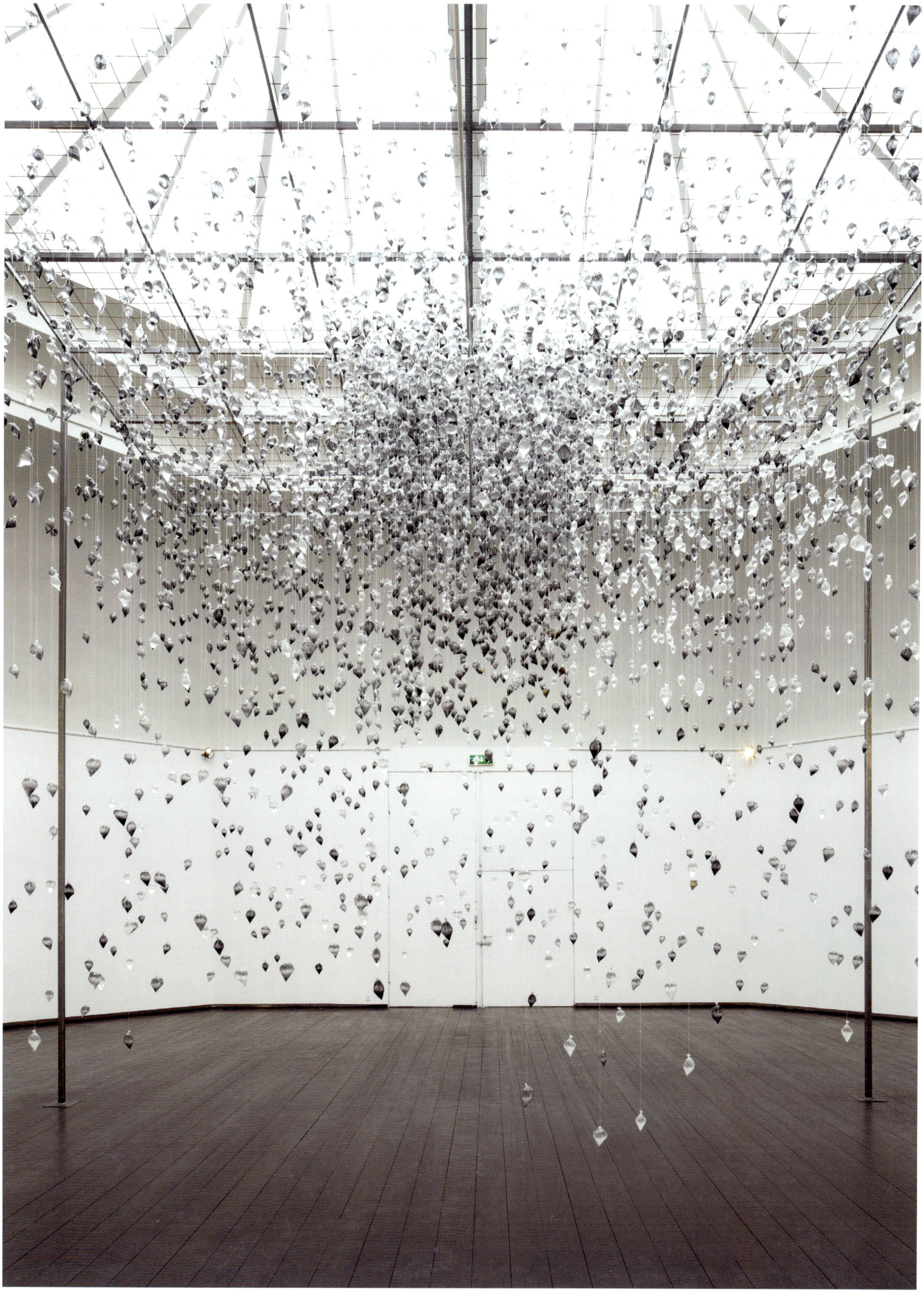

Bright Ugochukwu Eke, *Acid Rain*, Den Frie Center of Contemporary Art, Copenhagen/Kopenhagen

Foto/Photo: Anders Sune Berg

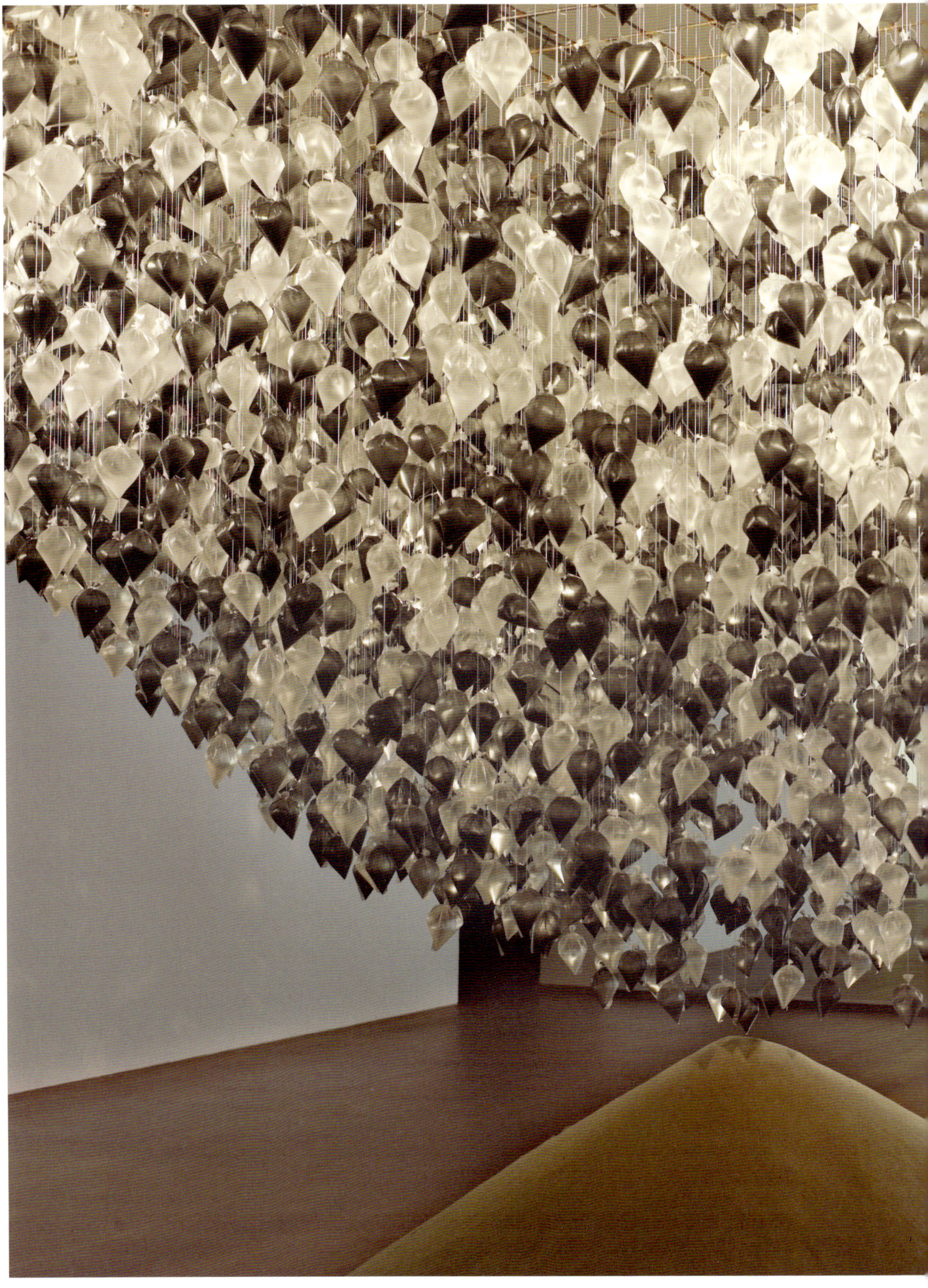

Bright Ugochukwu Eke, *Clouds-Earth Twist*, Ursula Blickle Stiftung, 2013

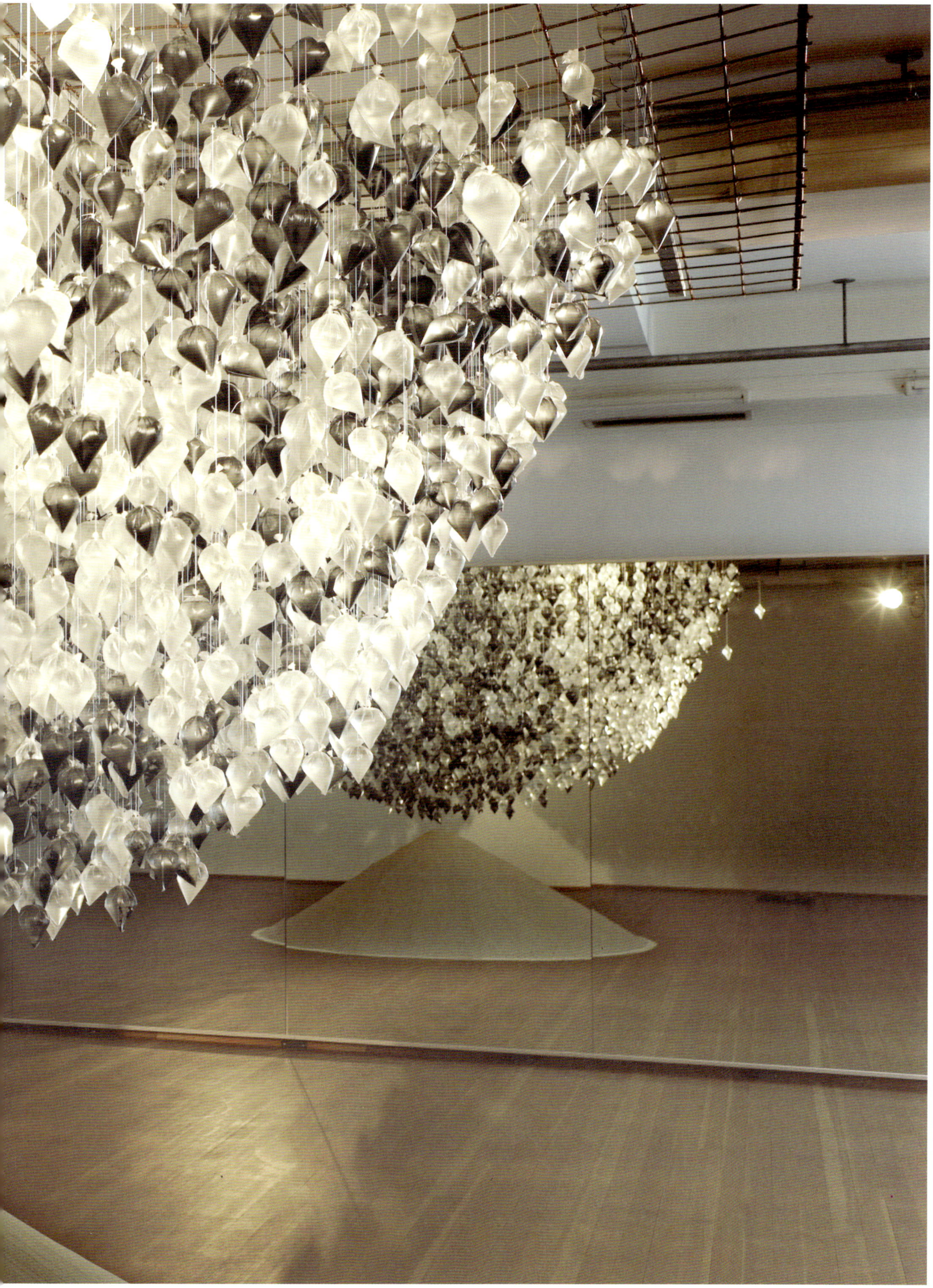

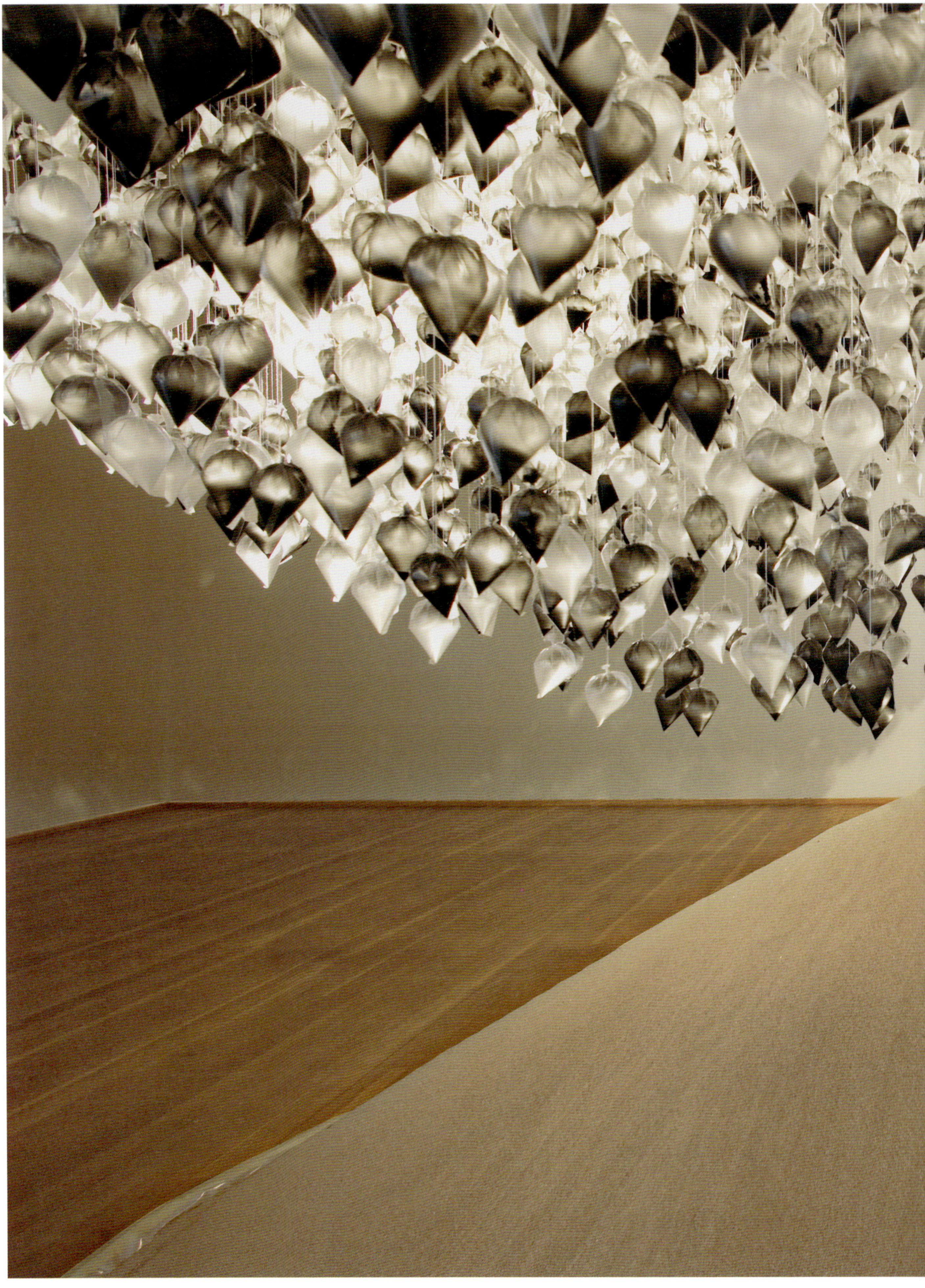

Bright Ugochukwu Eke, *Clouds-Earth Twist*, Ursula Blickle Stiftung, 2013

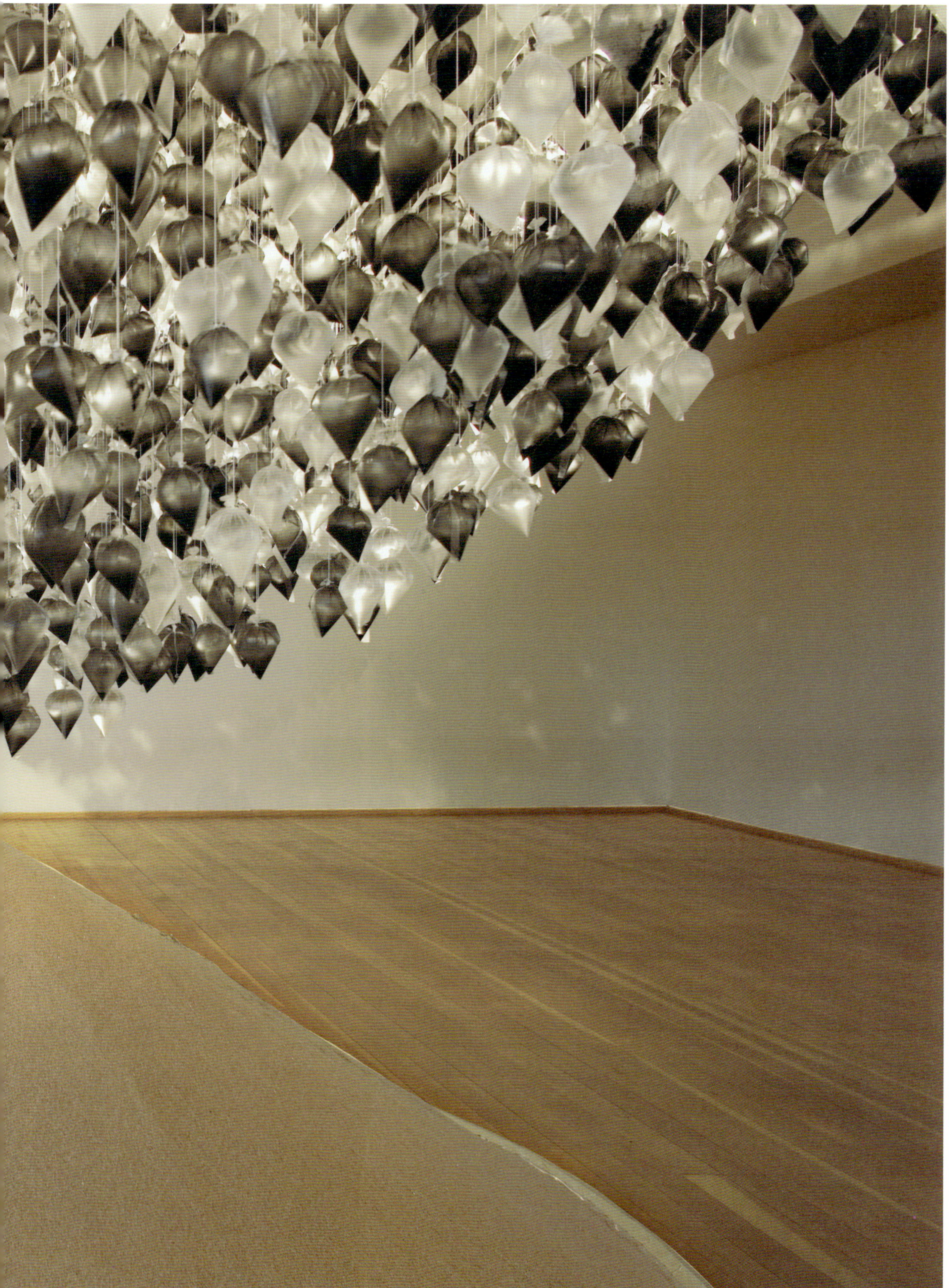

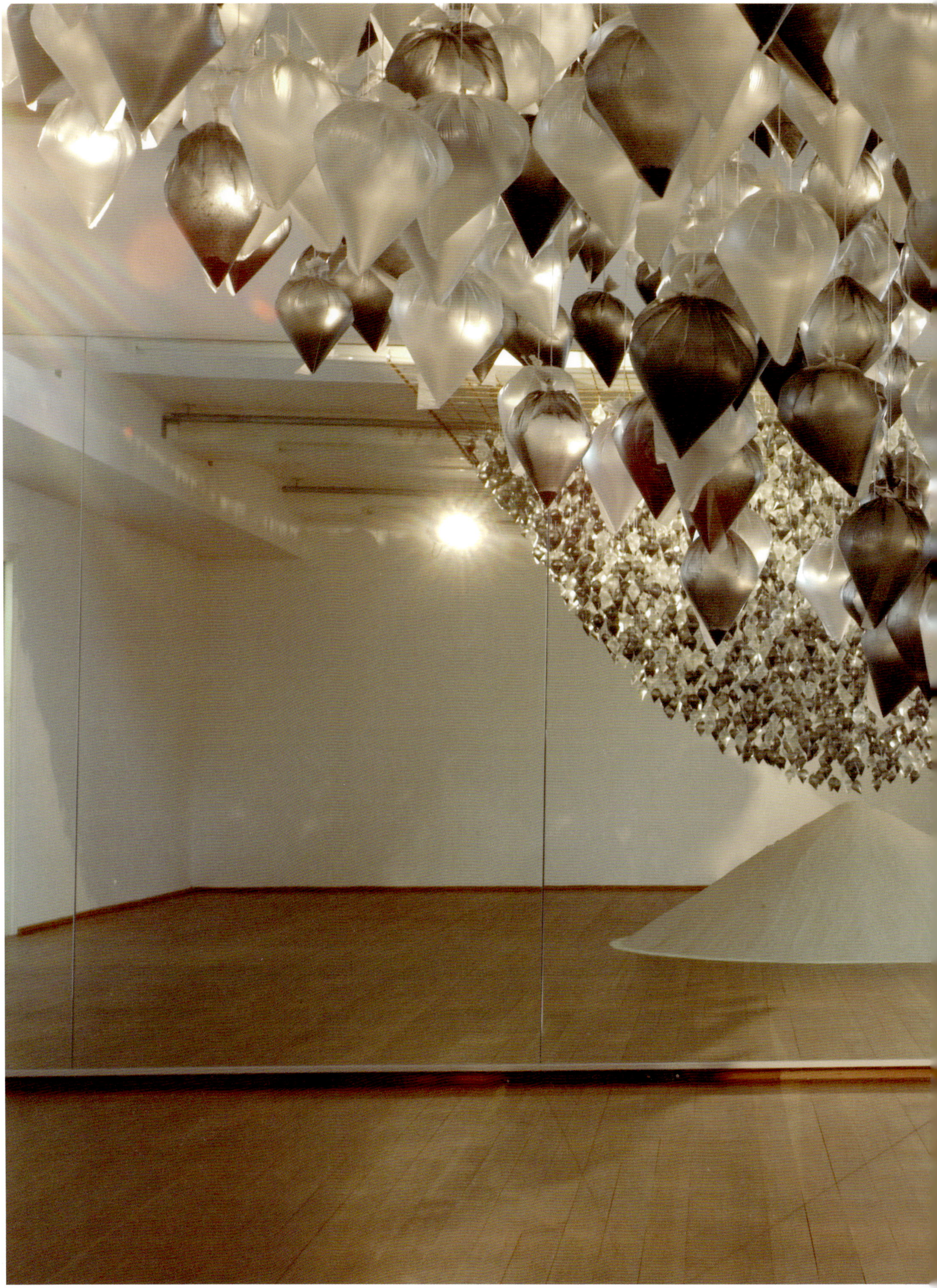

Bright Ugochukwu Eke, *Clouds-Earth Twist*, Ursula Blickle Stiftung, 2013

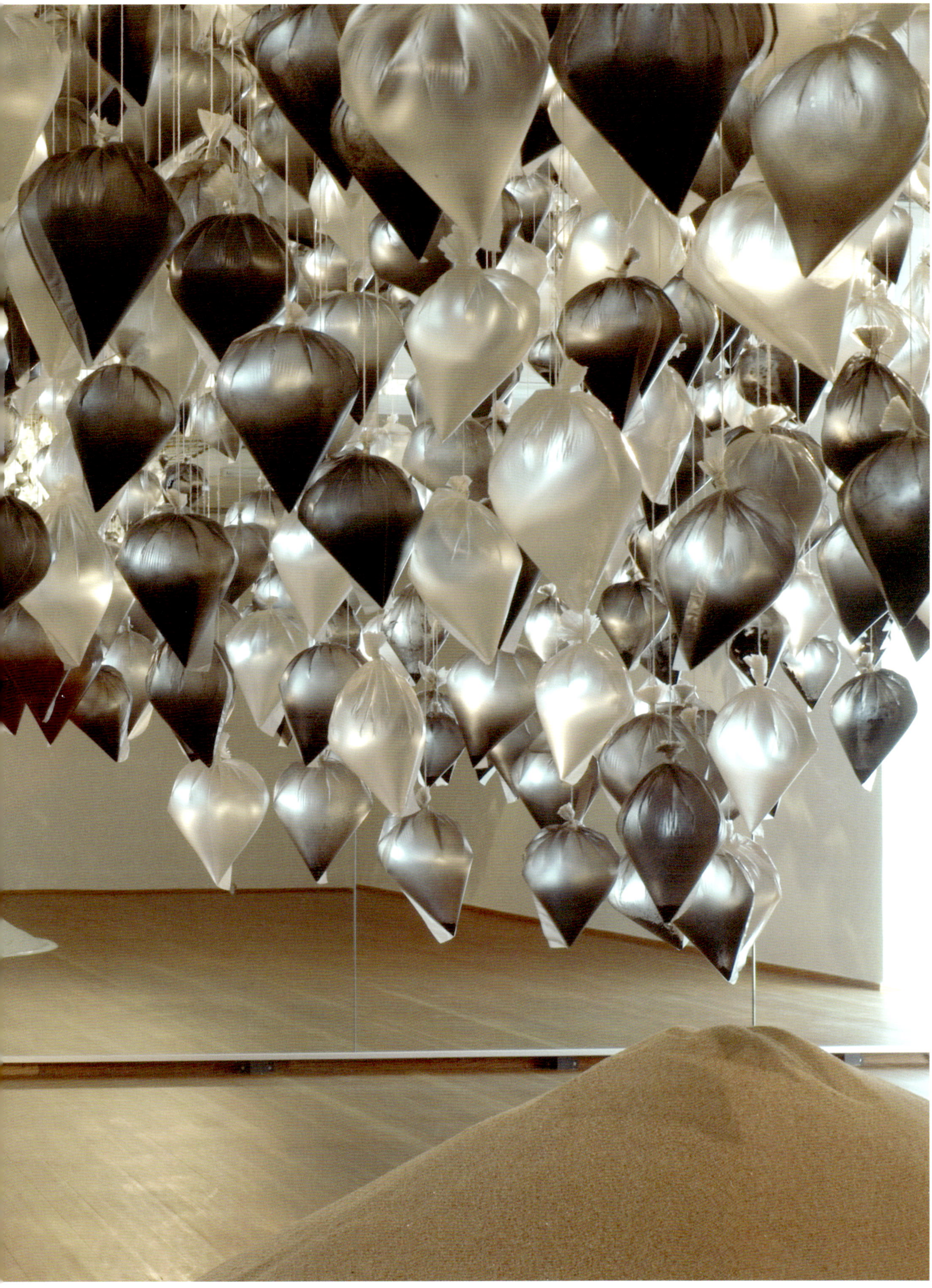

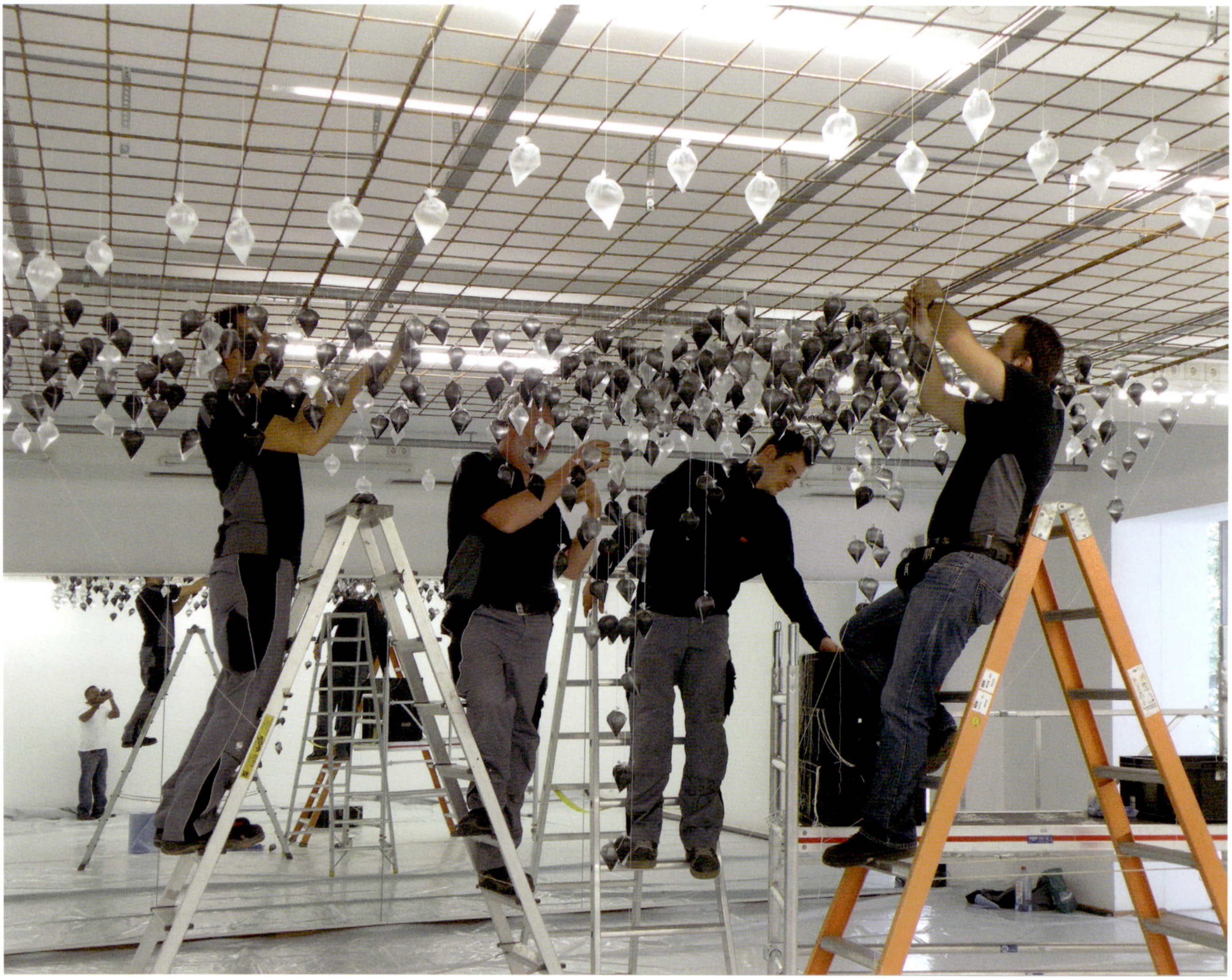

Aufbauteam der Ursula Blickle Stiftung beim Aufbau der Installation *Clouds-Earth Twist*

A team of the Ursula Blickle Stiftung is setting up the Clouds-Earth Twist installation

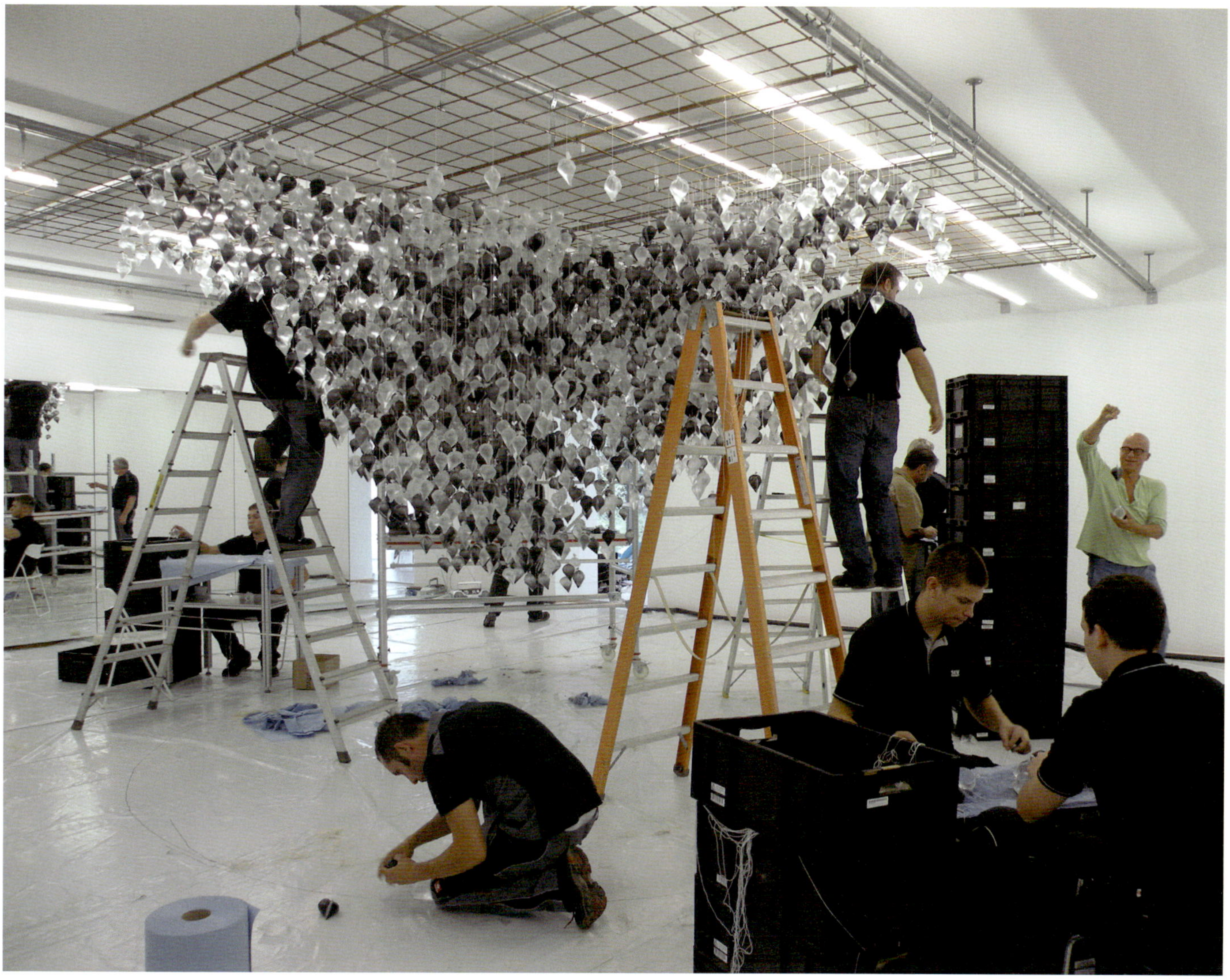

Aufbauteam der Ursula Blickle Stiftung beim Aufbau der Installation *Clouds-Earth Twist*

A team of the Ursula Blickle Stiftung is setting up the Clouds-Earth Twist installation

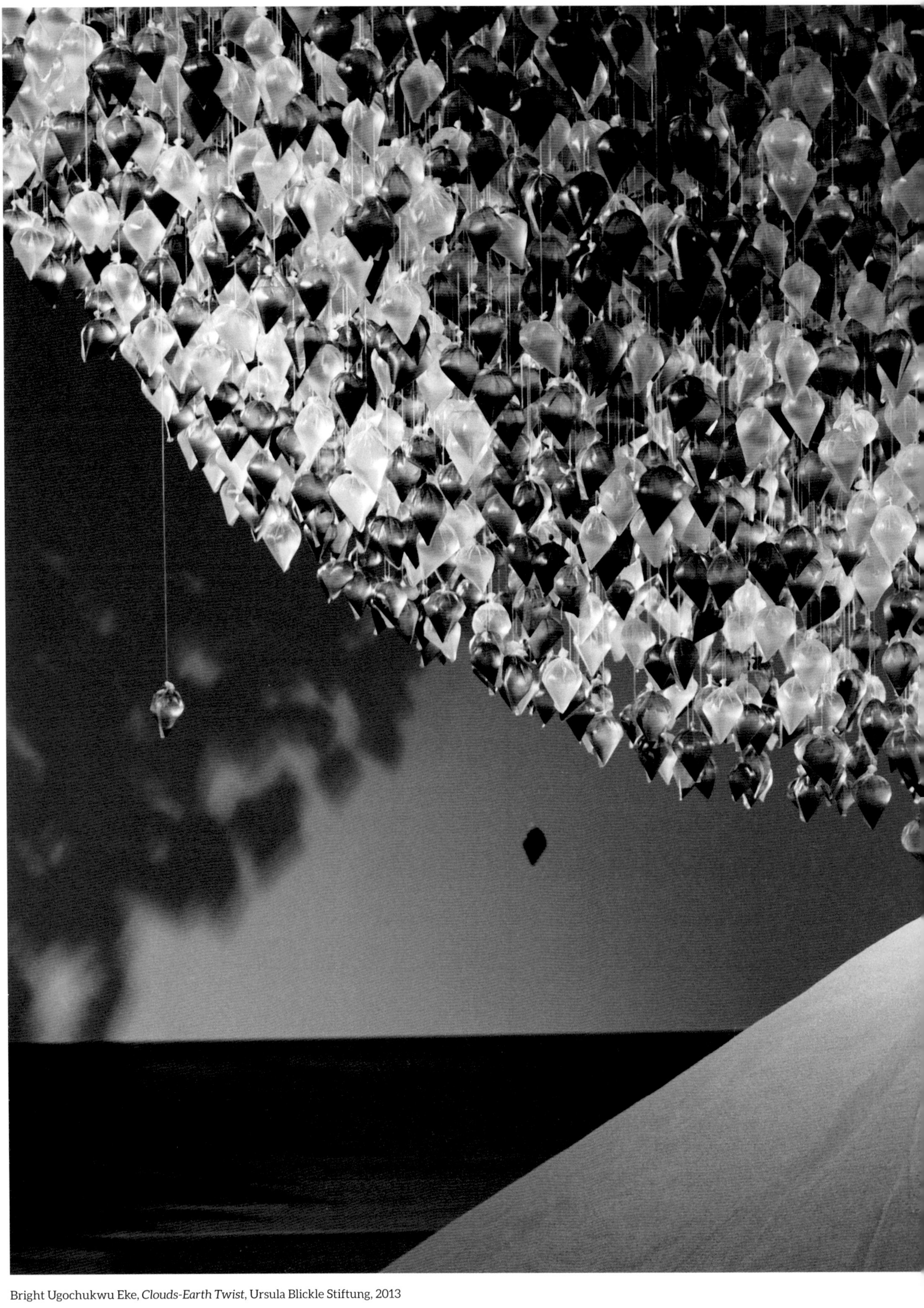

Bright Ugochukwu Eke, *Clouds-Earth Twist*, Ursula Blickle Stiftung, 2013

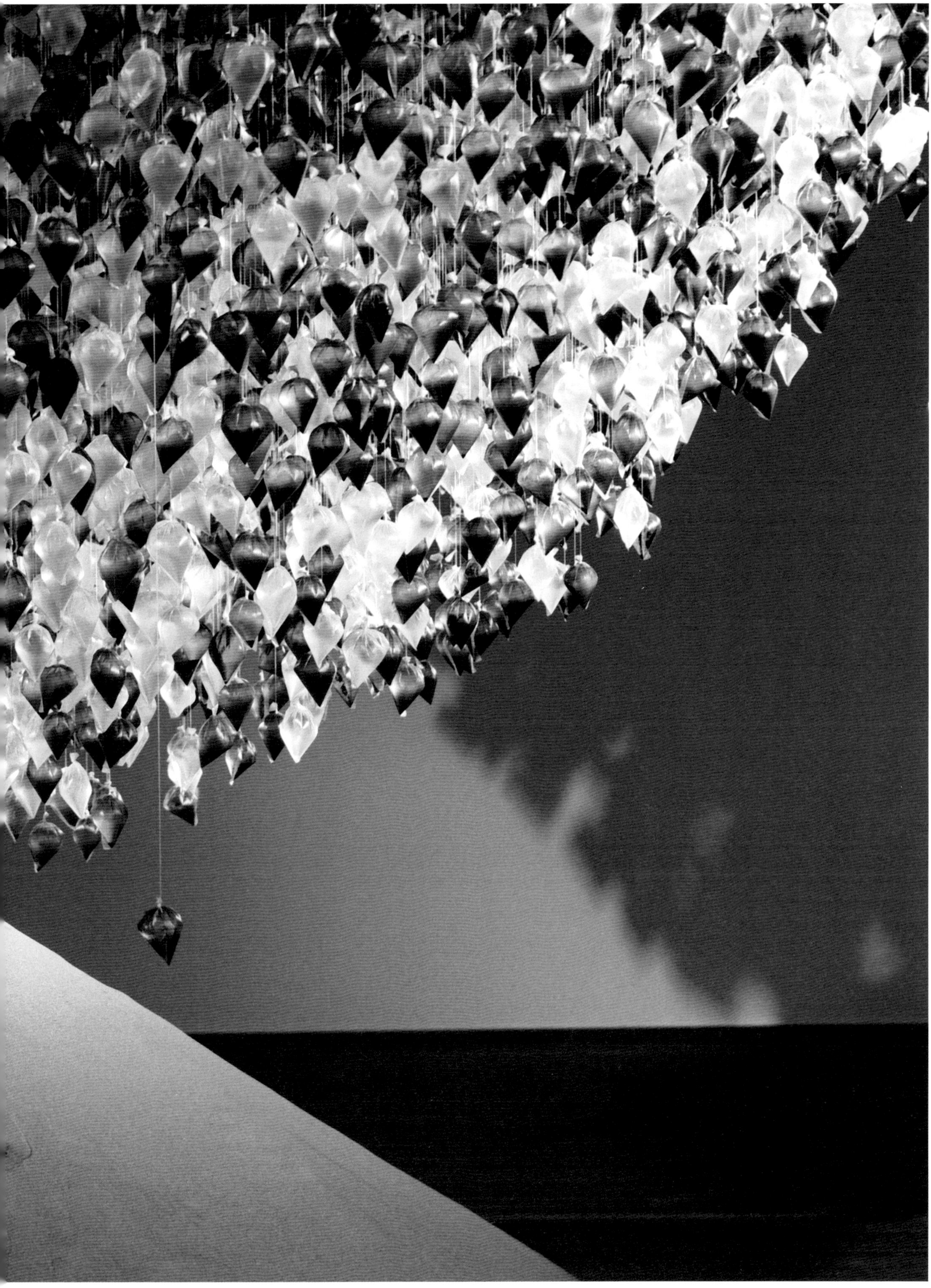

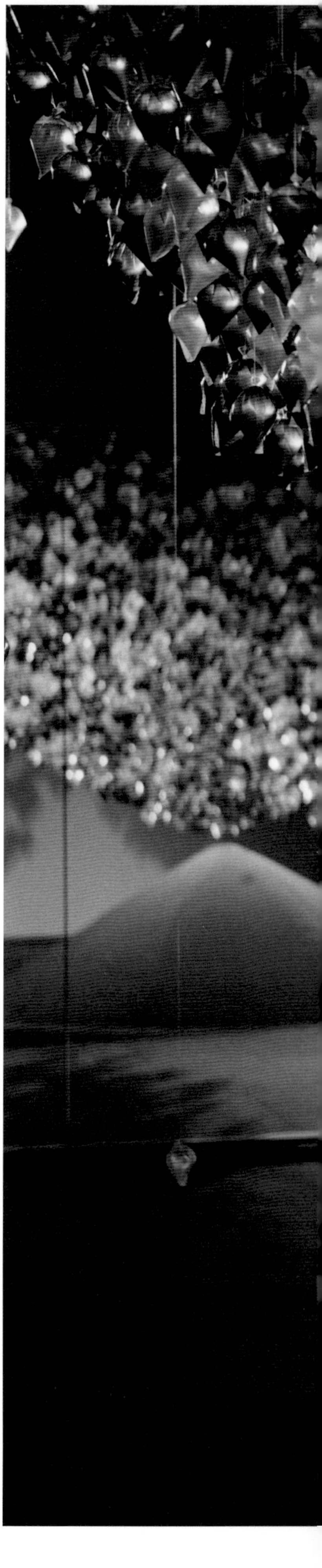

Bright Ugochukwu Eke, *Clouds-Earth Twist*, Ursula Blickle Stiftung, 2013

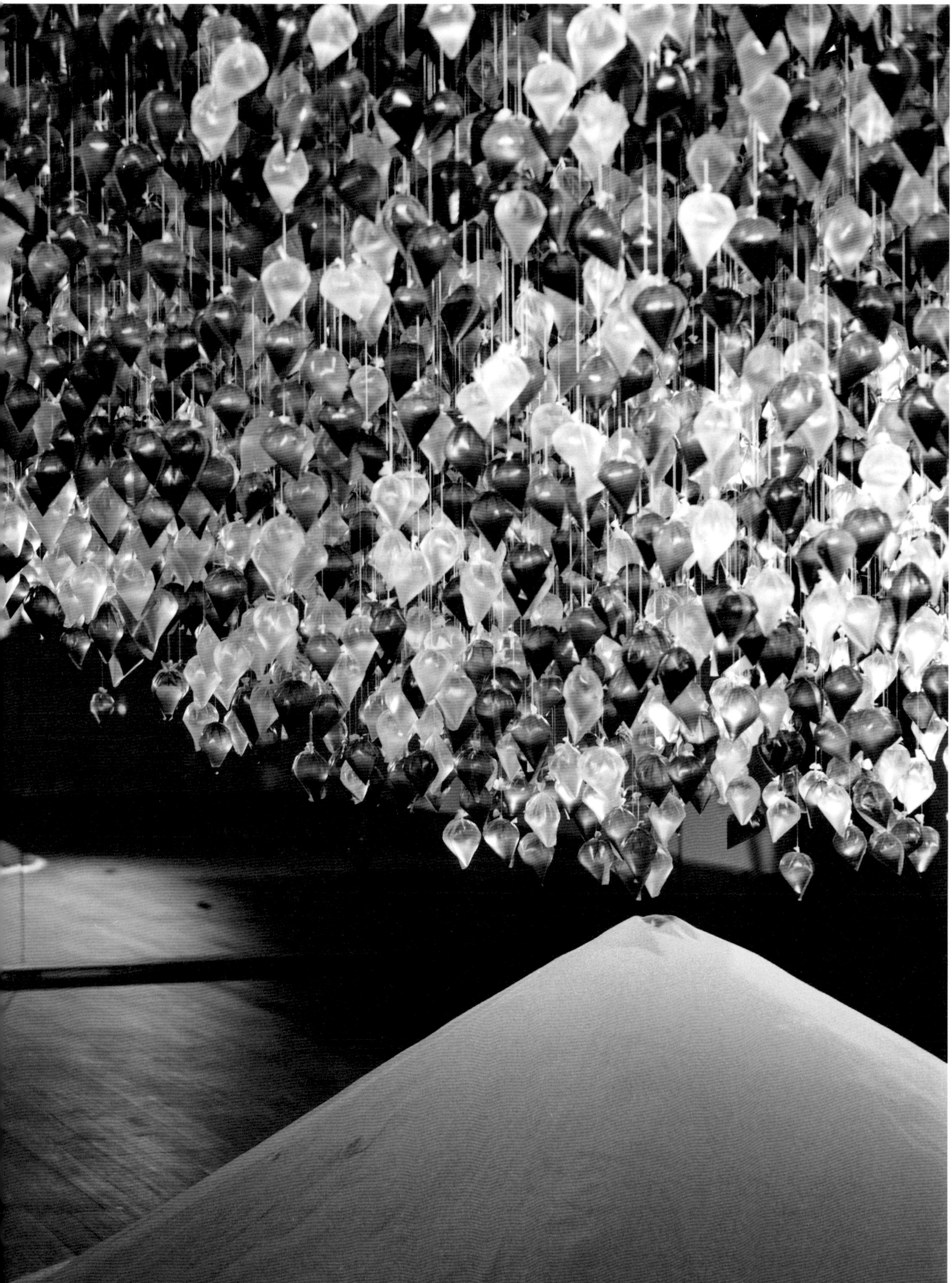

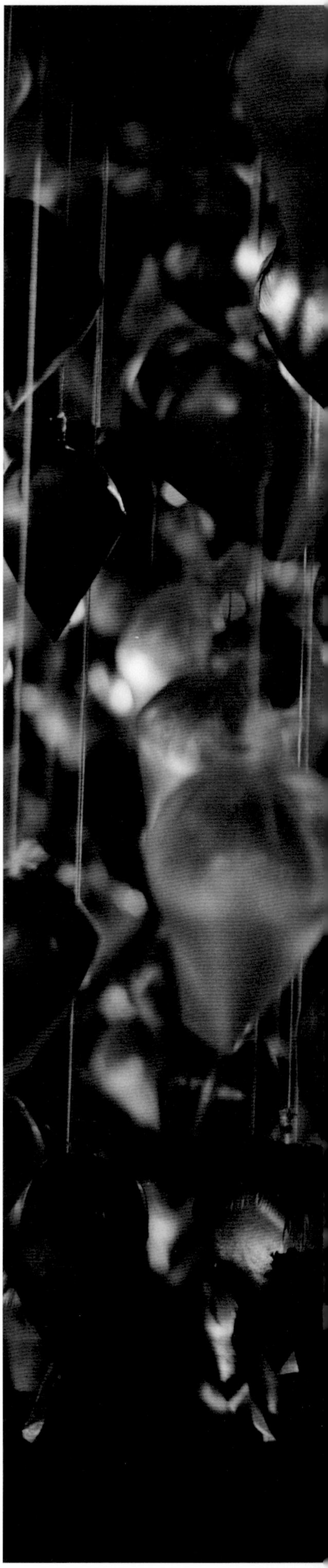

Bright Ugochukwu Eke, *Clouds-Earth Twist*, Ursula Blickle Stiftung, 2013

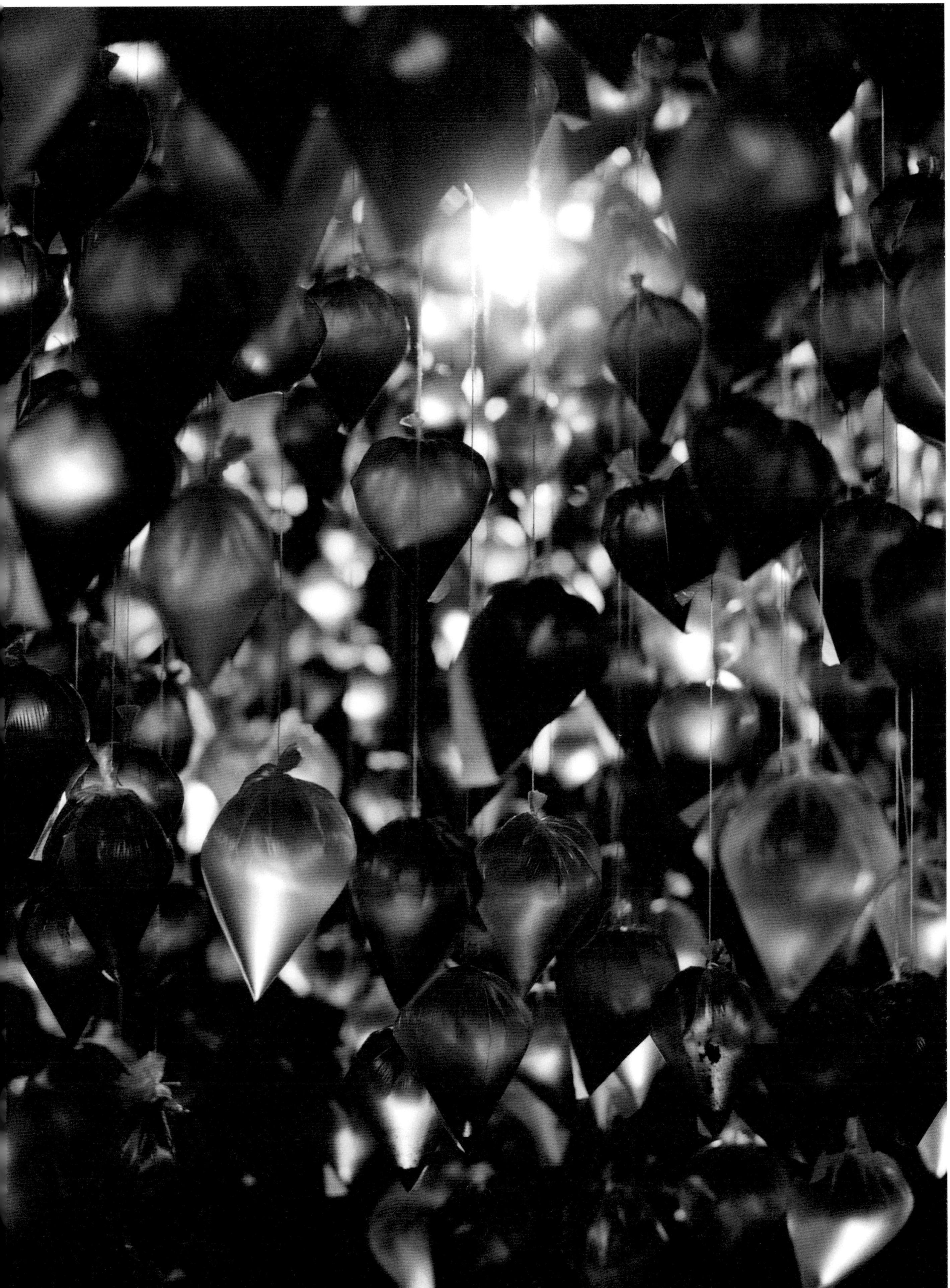

BIOGRAFIE
BRIGHT UGOCHUKWU EKE

Geboren 1976 in Mbaise, Nigeria, lebt derzeit in Los Angeles. Er erhielt seinen BA und MFA an der University of Nigeria, Nsukka.
Seit seinem Abschluss hat er zahlreiche Artist-in-Residence-Programme absolviert, z.B. in den Niederlanden, Trinidad und Tobago, den USA sowie Kolumbien. Seine Kunstwerke wurden in bereits in zahlreichen Ländern und Städten gezeigt, etwa in Algier, Durban, Lagos, London, New York, Richmond und Verona.
Bright Eke schafft an sozialen Aspekten orientierte Kunst. Es geht ihm dabei um die Erkundung der unterschiedlichen Aspekte des Umgangs der Menschen mit ihrer Umwelt. Er verwendet vor allem das Grundelement Wasser als Thema, nutzt es als künstlerisches Medium und fordert mit seinen Installationen den Rezipienten auf, sich mit dieser kostbaren Ressource in politischer, ethischer und ökologischer Hinsicht gedanklich auseinanderzusetzen. Bright Ekes Werk interpretiert das Abhängigkeitsverhalten unterschiedlicher Netzwerke, und kommentiert damit - konzeptionell oder/und körperlich - die Kultur und Umwelt.

„Als Künstler, setze ich mich vorwiegend mit dem Grundelement Wasser auseinander und verarbeite es in meinen Installationen. Ich untersuche die Bedeutung dieses künstlerischen Mediums und formuliere sowie visualisiere damit meine Gedanken zur Funktion menschlicher Verbindungen im Kontext zu ihrem Lebensraum. Als afrikanischer Künstler in einer globalen Gesellschaft bin ich daran interessiert das Element Wasser in einem globalen Kontext zu ergründen, in dem nicht nur Fragen zum Dasein der Menschen, sondern auch zur Umwelt und deren Behandlung durch den Menschen aufgeworfen werden. Je mehr ich mich mit dem Wasser auseinandersetze, desto häufiger entwickle ich neue Ideen und Prozesse zur Bewältigung der damit im Zusammenhang stehenden kritischen Probleme unserer Umwelt. Während dieses Vorgangs untersuche ich sowohl die historische und zeitgenössische Dimension des Wassers (in kultureller, sozialer, politischer und wirtschaftlicher Hinsicht) als auch ihre Auswirkung auf die Gesellschaft und die Umwelt. Die Materialien und Ideen stammen aus meiner Umwelt und werden mit ihr geformt. Sie stammen aus der Kultur(-Gesellschaft) und handeln von der Kultur(-Gesellschaft). Sie kommen vom Menschen und sind über die Menschen. „

BIOGRAPHY
BRIGHT UGOCHUKWU EKE

Born in 1976 in Mbaise, Nigeria, and currently lives in Los Angeles.
He received his BA and MFA from the University of Nigeria, Nsukka.
Since graduating he has held numerous artist residencies including ones in the Netherlands, Trinidad and Tobago and Colombia. His works have been shown in cities as varied as Algiers, Durban, Lagos, London, New York, Richmond and Verona.
Bright Eke creates socially oriented art, exploring the ways in which people interact with their environments. Using water as a theme and medium, he challenges viewers to think about this precious resource politically, ethically, and ecologically. Eke's work looks at the interdependence of various networks, and therefore comments on culture and the environment as much as it derives from them — conceptually or physically.

„As an artist, I explore ideas about water in my installations. I search for the meaning of this medium, and use its language in articulating my ideas on the functions and dysfunctions of human connections to one another and the surrounding Earth. As an African artist in a global society, I am interested in exploring water in ways that examine global, human, and environmental issues. The more I work with water, the more I discover new ideas and processes addressing these critical issues. Throughout this process, I study the historical and contemporary dimensions of water (cultural, social, political and economic), and their implications on society and the physical environment. The materials and ideas I work with are from the environment and about the environment. They are from the culture/society and about the culture/society. They come from the people and are about the people."

AUSBILDUNG /EDUCATION
M.F.A University of Nigeria, Nsukka (2007)
B.A. University of Nigeria, Nsukka (2002)

ZUKÜNFTIGE PROJEKTE /FUTURE PROJECTS

2013

The Water of Life: Artistic Expressions, Fedex Global Center, University of North Carolina.

High Trash, Robert Hull Fleming Museum, Burlington, Vermont.

PERSONALAUSSTELLUNGEN /SOLO EXHIBITIONS

2013

Clouds-Earth Twist, Ursula Blickle Foundation, Kraichtal

2008

Water and Me; Art in Public Space - Trinidad and Tobago

2007

Environ-Scope: Goethe Institute, Lagos, Nigeria

GRUPPENAUSSTELLUNGEN (Auswahl) / SELECTED GROUP EXHIBITIONS

2012

Environment and Object, Recent African Art, Middlebury College Museum of Art, Vermont

2011

Don't Panic: Goethe Institute, Durban, South Africa

Environment and Object, Recent African Art, Anderson Gallery, Virginia Commonwealth University, Virginia

Water and Waste; Åland Island Art Museum, Aland Island

2010

Neither Here Nor There; JAMM: Contemporary Art Exhibition, London.

What's the Matter? Onirica 2010, Grand Guard Palace, Verona, Italy.

The woods that see and hear, s´-Hertogenbosch, Netherlands.

2009

The 2nd Thessaloniki Biennale of Contemporary Art, "PRAXIS: Art in Times of Uncertainty", Greece.

1st International Festival of Contemporary Art (FIAC of Algiers), National Museum of Modern and Contemporary Art of Algiers.

RETHINK: THE IMPLICIT, Contemporary Art and Climate Change: Den Frie Center for Contemporary Art, Copenhagen, Denmark.

All Barnsley Diversity Festival, South Yorkshire, UK.

Stichting Art in Redlight, Amsterdam.

TASTE 2009: Root Division, San Francisco, USA.

CODE SHARE, 10 Biennales, 20 Artists, 5 Continents, International Exhibition, Vilnius, Lithuania.

2008

Echo Wanted: Galerie Karsten Greve, Paris.

Experimental Frontiers: society through the eyes of South African and Nigerian artists; Cape Town, South Africa.

WATER: Delight and Misery; Ifa Gallery, Stuttgart, Ifa Gallery Berlin, Germany.

Art, Migration, and Identity: International Exhibition for the International Festival of Art in Arnhem – Netherlands.

2007

Art, Ecology and the Politics of Change - Sharjah Biennial 8, United Arab Emirates.

Trans-Cape Contemporary African Art Exhibition, Cape Town, South Africa.

M.F.A, Final (Studio and thesis) Exhibition, WATER: Medium, Process and Idea.

For Sculpture, Ana Gallery, University of Nigeria, Nsukka.

2006

ACP (African, Caribbean and Pacific) Festival, Santa Domingo, Antilles.

DAK'ART, 7th Biennial of Contemporary African Art, IFAN Musuem, Dakar, Senegal.

M.F.A. (first) Exhibition, Ana Gallery, University of Nigeria, Nsukka.

3rd International Conference - Exhibition on Modern Art in Nigeria, University of Nigeria, Nsukka.

2005

5th Biennial Exhibition of Pan African Circle of Artists, National Museum, Enugu.

45th Founders Day Anniversary Exhibition, University of Nigeria, Nsukka.

IMPRESSUM

Dieser Katalog erscheint anlässlich der Ausstellung Acid Rain vom 15. September bis 20. Oktober 2013 in der Ursula Blickle Stiftung, Kraichtal.

Ursula Blickle Stiftung
Mühlweg 18
D-76703 Kraichtal-Unteröwisheim
www.ursula-blickle-stiftung.de

Herausgeber: Alfred Weidinger für Ursula Blickle Stiftung
Grafikdesign: Dieter Auracher

Druck und Bindung: SEW-EURODRIVE GmbH & Co KG

Jovis Verlag GmbH
Kurfürstenstraße 15/16
D-10785 Berlin
www.jovis.de

ISBN 978-3-86859-291-7

Bibliografische Information der Deutschen Nationalbibliothek: Die Deutsche Nationalbibliothek verzeichnet diese Publikation in der Deutschen Nationalbibliografie; detaillierte bibliografische Daten sind im Internet über http://dnb.de abrufbar.

IMPRINT

This catalogue is published on the occasion of the exhibition Acid Rain, September 15 until October 20, 2013, Ursula Blickle Foundation, Kraichtal

Ursula Blickle Stiftung
Mühlweg 18
D-76703 Kraichtal-Unteröwisheim
www.ursula-blickle-stiftung.de

Editor: Alfred Weidinger for Ursula Blickle Foundation
Graphic Design: Dieter Auracher

Printed and bound by SEW-EURODRIVE GmbH & Co KG

Jovis Verlag GmbH
Kurfürstenstraße 15/16
D-10785 Berlin
www.jovis.de

ISBN 978-3-86859-291-7

Bibliographic information published by the Deutsche Nationalbibliothek: The Deutsche Nationalbibliothek lists this publication in the Deutsche Nationalbibliografie; detailed bibliographic data are available in the Internet at http://dnb.de.